HARVESTING THE DREAM

HARVESTING THE DREAM

THE RAGS-TO-RICHES TALE OF THE SUTTER HOME WINERY

KATE HEYHOE
and
STANLEY HOCK

WILEY

JOHN WILEY & SONS, INC.

For general information on our other products and services please contact our
Customer Care Department within the United States at (800) 762-2974, outside
the United States at (317) 572-3993 or fax (317) 572-4002.

Wiley also publishes its books in a variety of electronic formats. Some content that
appears in print may not be available in electronic books. For more information
about Wiley products, visit our web site at *www.Wiley.com*.

ISBN 0-471-42972-4

Printed in the United States of America

10 9 8 7 6 5 4 3 2 1

To Fred McMillin, wine scholar and gentleman, and to Thomas Way, wine lover and best friend.—KH

Contents

Preface

In a millennium already characterized by "infectious greed" (as Fed chief Alan Greenspan has called it), the Enron scandal, silicon smashups, dot-com crashes, unthinkable terrorism, and a U.S. war in Iraq, the Trinchero family winery illustrates a remarkable and upbeat American business success story—though it's not without plenty of ups, downs, fortuitous accidents, blind trust, brilliant marketing, savvy smarts, hidden drama—and even a bit of dumb luck.

In just four decades, a humble mom-and-pop operation grew into America's fourth largest winery, and today Trinchero Family Estates (TFE) is not just the parent company of Sutter Home wines, it's also the second largest independent, family-run winery in the United States.

The Trincheros and Sutter Home are to the beverage industry what Herb Kelleher and Southwest Airlines have been to the travel industry. Both companies understand what consumers want, and neither is ashamed to give it to them. In 1967, Southwest Airlines revolutionized the airline industry with no frills, affordable travel, stewardesses in hot pants, and hearts painted on planes. Less than two decades later, Sutter Home sent tremors through the wine world with its own surprising success: a sweet, pink, chillable wine called White Zinfandel.

Its label reads in full: Sutter Home White Zinfandel, bottled by Trinchero Family Estates (TFE). Bob Trinchero, its creator, calls it the longest overnight success in history.

You won't see it on most white-tablecloth-restaurant wine lists, in *Wine Spectator* awards, or served at the Oscars. Instead, you'll find it in the wine and beer aisles of supermarkets, drugstores, and mini-marts: 750-milliliter bottles of fruity, pastel pink wine, priced at just $4.99 and often sold for less (1.5-liter bottles sell for $7.99 to $8.99). If it hadn't been for a fortuitous accident—a stuck fermentation—Sutter Home White Zinfandel would never have become even a blip on the enological radar screen. This is a rare story of a family that still runs a business based on professional and personal integrity, with employees they consider more like nieces and nephews than workers. If, as some believe, Robert Mondavi is flamboyant and flashy, then the Trincheros are the antithesis. Within the glitzy, chichi atmosphere of Napa Valley, the Trincheros stand out because they are genuine, generous, self-effacing, and humble. Unlike other family vintners, they prefer not to be in the limelight; they avoid self-aggrandizement, shun flamboyance, and retain the simple values of 1950s America, when Mario and Mary Trinchero were raising Bob, Roger, and Vera, the current scions of the family estate.

The Trinchero family story is more than just a wine-industry chronicle. It illuminates the best aspects of the American dream—that with hard work, a willingness to take risks and defy well-rooted conventions, an understanding that business prosperity is measured by sales and not ego, and an invisible sensor set to beep at the slightest hint of opportunity, even unassuming owners can achieve phenomenal success. The road to success in this case wasn't paved by Harvard MBAs, elaborate business plans, angel investors, or publicly held stocks.

Still, without their creation of Sutter Home White Zinfandel, the Trinchero family would likely have been a mere trifling footnote in wine history. Prior to the near-accidental discovery of White Zinfandel, their traditional wines hardly paid the bills. White Zinfandel's sudden boom surprised everyone, though not always positively. Critics didn't just snub the wine (dubbing it "soda pop with a kick"); many were actively repulsed by it, as if this wine were an affront to the entire American wine industry.

Ironically, it was the wine's uniquely non-European characteristics that catapulted it to legendary success. While critics shunned White Zinfandel, consumers craved it. With palates attuned to soft drinks and Big Macs, Americans slurped up 2 million cases of it in 1987, making Sutter Home White Zinfandel America's best-selling wine. At last! Here was the wine consumers had been silently waiting for: It was light, fresh, sweet, pretty, unintimidating, and best served chilled. For many Americans, it was the first wine they actually enjoyed drinking.

CHALLENGES

Yet, right now, the Trincheros' future success is far from guaranteed. In opening up an untapped market for White Zinfandel and other fruity, affordable wines, they ensured their own profits in the "fighting varietal" segment of $3 to $7 wines, but soon had to share that market with some fierce competitors. Today, the only way for the Trincheros to grow as a winery is to capture the lion's share of another glutted market, that of superpremium $7 to $14 wines.

For decades, Sutter Home Winery was a notably underwhelming business, muddling along while such competitors as Robert Mondavi, Gallo, and Beringer were solidly building their empires. Founding themselves on award-winning wines good enough to compete with fine European vintages, Mondavi and Beringer, in particular, established their reputations as superpremium and ultra-premium winemakers and were able to command higher prices for their wines. When the Trincheros illuminated the demand for inexpensive wines acceptable to popular tastes, their Napa Valley neighbors dived right in, knocking out competitive lower-end wines without doing damage to their own brands.

Not so with the Trincheros. Both consumers and critics have pigeonholed the Sutter Home brand as a lower-end concept, a wine not worth more than $4.99 a bottle. Even though Napa vintners know the Trinchero family has the technical ability to produce fine wines, the Trincheros face an uphill battle that requires a change in public perception. Their biggest hurdle is not in crafting premium wines, which they are indeed doing, but in reversing an image. Consequently, since 1990, the Trinchero family has struck out with a diverse range of new wine products and aggressive marketing plans, all targeted at distinguishing Trinchero Family Estates as a wine company with class and Sutter Home as merely one brand within the company. The question is: Have they entered the fine-wine market too late, with too little in the way of global resources and image cachet?

If you talk to the Trincheros, they don't think so. They're confident that they know the consumer, that they understand the business, and that without the profit-directed constraints restricting a publicly held corporation, they can take the same types of risks that led to their quick growth and ultimate success as the fourth largest American winemaker. But they do admit that globalization and consolidation are forcing them to remap their strategies. Today, TFE is no longer the fourth largest winery, the boom of White Zinfandel having leveled off. But nevertheless, whenever current measures of sales or volumes are tallied (which fluctuate as rapidly as television network ratings), Trinchero Family Estates is generally considered the sixth largest winery.

As the gentle older brother Bob Trinchero (now chairman and CEO) will assuredly tell you, they know how to craft fine wines and are doing so already with their homage to their father Mario, the Trinchero brand. For Trinchero Family Estates, the future is ripe with a new image, new products, and quality wines comparable to, if not better than, those of their competitors. This is the story of where they've come from, their rise to success, and the unique challenges this pioneering family faces within the "New Napa."

WHAT YOU WILL FIND IN THIS BOOK

In writing this book, we had several specific goals in mind:

- Showcase the rags-to-riches success story of a unique American family business
- Illustrate how they've founded their success on honesty, strong moral values, and philanthropy
- Outline the steps the Trincheros are taking to maintain or expand their profits
- Document a case study of a large family winery hovering between consolidated corporate giants and Napa Valley's artisanal wineries
- Identify the global and consumer trends shaping the future of the wine industry
- Illuminate the U.S. wine industry as a prosperous commerce sector facing increasing competition from imports and globalization

Today's consumer has more wine choices than ever before, better wines to choose from, and more affordable wines of good quality pouring in from around the globe. But a winery's ability to get its brands to the market shelf is increasingly challenging, especially for independent wineries. Few consumers realize the degree to which homogenization and consolidation are affecting their options for wines, both positively and negatively. After reading this book, you will probably never look at your supermarket wine aisle in the same way again!

This book consists of three parts, containing quotes, anecdotes, and supporting material from Trinchero family members, employees, Napa neighbors, wine-colleagues, critics, and wine-industry experts.

Part 1: "The Move Out West," traces the history of the Trinchero family's entrance into wine making, from Italian vineyards to New York speakeasies and, ultimately, to Napa Valley.

In 1948, Mario Trinchero and his brother John revived the old Sutter Home Winery in Napa. Even before this, around the turn of the century, their father, Luigi, had owned a vineyard in Italy. Later, Luigi's daughter Diana migrated to New York City and married an Italian, fondly known as "the Little Gangster." Together they ran a speakeasy in Manhattan, whose profits allowed Diana to bring her family from Italy to New York. Mario and John assisted their father in making Prohibition and post-Prohibition-era wine. Then, in 1945, John visited Napa Valley as a buyer for a large wine company. The region's beauty captivated him. With a partner, John bought the once-prosperous Sutter Home Winery. The partner soon quit the project, and Mario Trinchero, at age 49, took his place. He brought with him his wife, Mary, and children, Bob, Roger, and Vera.

"We pulled into the winery," recalls eldest son Bob (who was 12 at the time), "which was a dilapidated old barn that hadn't been operated since before Prohibition. It had been abandoned and was waist high in weeds in the front, with dirt floors and no electricity. My mother started to cry. We came from midtown Manhattan, where we had a pretty nice lifestyle, so we couldn't understand why my dad would bring us to a place like this."

The Sutter Home Winery, prior to the Trincheros' purchase, reflects the early history of Napa, a wine industry devastated by the 1906 San Francisco earthquake and fire, the banking panic of 1907, in which wine-drinking foreigners left the country in search of jobs, a killer frost in 1916, and, ultimately, Prohibition, the final straw that broke the original Sutter Home's wine production.

If it hadn't been for New York mayor Fiorello La Guardia, California grapes would have died out entirely. He engineered a loophole that allowed households to make up to 200 gallons of wine per year. Railroad cars of thick-skinned, durable grapes crossed the country from Napa to New York. After Prohibition was repealed and World War II ended, an entrepreneurial zeal revitalized the wine industry, and the Trinchero brothers leaped right in.

From 1948 to the mid-1960s, the story follows the Trincheros through the ups and downs of being a small business, raising a family, and working together, all amid events that were slowly developing Napa into the center of American wine.

Part 2: "Eureka! Liquid Gold and the Blush Rush," continues the saga of the Trincheros and Sutter Home through their years of phenomenal growth. By 1960, Bob Trinchero had become the family winemaker. During this period, Bob discovered Amador County and its uniquely American grape, Zinfandel. In 1971, Bob released his 1968

Sutter Home Amador County Zinfandel, which became an instant success. "It was the best wine I had ever made," Bob recalls. "It put us on the map, a small map, perhaps, but a fine-wine map." As a result, Bob made a radical decision—that Sutter Home should become a Zinfandel-only winery.

Competitors jumped on the "big-zin" bandwagon. To make an even heartier Zinfandel, Bob employed a technique in which some of the juice is drawn off right after crushing, intensifying the wine. The result was a wonderfully rich red wine, but it left Bob with 550 gallons of pale juice that he turned into a dry, but mediocre "white" Zinfandel, one that was not readily accepted. Then a fortuitous accident occurred: a stuck fermentation (the wine fermented before all the sugar was converted to alcohol), leaving about 2 percent residual sugar and a pale pink tinge. Bob tried to correct the process, but failed, so he bottled it anyway. As a result, in 1975, the Sutter Home White Zinfandel we know today was born. It sold in unprecedented numbers, and with it came the Trinchero family's surge to become America's fourth largest winemaker.

Between 1981 and 1986, Sutter Home's production of White Zinfandel grew from 25,000 cases to more than 1.3 million, and the winery continues to be the leading seller of White Zinfandel today. But even as the "Blush Years" were peaking, the Trincheros knew this was the time to compete in newly expanding markets: Chardonnay and superpremium wines. By 1998, they proudly announced the release of a wine honoring their father Mario, the Trinchero brand of ultrapremium wines.

Throughout their expansion, the Trincheros never compromised their values. Without intending to, they became corporate role models because of their employee programs, their philanthropic efforts, and their genuine caring for the community.

In Part 3: "Globalization and the New Napa," we segue to the millennium. Where is the California wine world headed? Will the Trincheros be leading, lagging, or treading water? Sutter Home's amazing success has a downside: It became typecast among consumers as a producer of affordable, everyday wines, but not of wines in the higher tiers. In typical Trinchero fashion, the family has set about to change that perception.

White Zinfandel taught the Trincheros two important lessons that guide their actions today: (1) It pays to break with tradition, and (2) it's best to satisfy consumer tastes, not your own. In doing so, they've actively shaped the character of the wine industry.

At the same time, the wine industry itself, a weak economy, and global corporate competition are shaping the ways Trinchero Family Estates does business. A possible sale in 2000 to Constellation Brands, today the world's largest wine company, did not go through, but it sent a ripple of reactions throughout Trinchero Family Estates.

Today, the combined forces of globalization and consolidation hammer away at small, medium, and independent wineries. The Trincheros' family winery faces the same challenges as other companies, but because of its unique size, it stands a better chance than most of remaining independent— if that's what the family wants. The senior Trincheros look fondly toward eventual retirement, but, leaving aside Roger's teenage children, only two members of the next generation appear to be viable candidates for continuing the family's leadership. Bob, Roger, and Vera have seriously considered selling out, but they've rejected all offers to date. The future of Trinchero Family Estates is unknown, but one thing is certain: If and when they take steps to seriously alter the company structure, the wine industry—and consumers—will feel the impact, whichever direction they choose.

Acknowledgments

Thanks to the people of Napa Valley who shared their thoughts on the many topics in this book. I'm particularly grateful to veteran wine historian Fred McMillin, wine columnist for *Global Gourmet* (globalgourmet.com) these many years. Darrell Corti and Dan Berger, in particular, shared many valuable insights and opinions. Mille grazie to Evelyn Lambert, my godmother, who gave me my first taste of wine and never poured a bad glass. My mother gets big thanks for her endless encouragement and caring. Thomas Way made this a better book, as he does with all my books, and he always reminds me that the glass is half full. Thanks to Cyril Penn, editor at *Wine Business,* for giving me access to their fine publications and archives, and to Stan Wakefield for inviting me to join this project. I'm especially thankful to my editor Matt Holt for having the vision to bring this story to publication, and for his support and enthusiasm. And finally, thanks to the Trinchero and the Torres families, for their honesty, cooperation, and willingness to openly share their lives.   —KH

PART ONE

A WINERY IN
THE WEST

1

The Family

A portrait of the late Mario Trinchero hangs in the dining room at the restored Victorian mansion next to the Sutter Home Winery, now called Trinchero Family Estates. With thinning hair but still a youthful appearance for a man then in his seventies, he sports a black turtleneck and black jacket, casual yet sophisticated. He could be a Hollywood agent or a Wall Street investor, but he's not. He's a humble man who lived a true rags-to-riches story, staking everything on the quintessential American dream.

In the portrait, Mario's velvety black eyes gaze directly back at the viewer, as though he's still alive, vibrant, and in control of the winery where he first toiled more than 50 years ago. Perhaps, through his children, he is.

At first glance, you would hardly know that Bob, Roger, and Vera Trinchero are siblings, the children of Mario and Mary Trinchero. They're so dissimilar, they could be any three people randomly picked from a crowd, except for their eyes: luminous, ebony, inkwell eyes. Mario's eyes.

At six feet three inches, the lean and athletic Roger, youngest of the three, stands several heads over both Bob and Vera. Now in his mid–fifties, Roger played college football. If a movie were to be made of the Trincheros' lives, the actor-playwright Sam Shepard would be an ideal candidate to play the role of Roger: trim, fit, with an enigmatic flow of thought and emotions lurking just below the surface. A veteran of Vietnam, Roger has been described as a playboy and hellion in his younger days, and a good guy who settled into being a smart, kind, and loyal employer. He was the first Trinchero to graduate from college. Today, he's president of Trinchero Family Estates.

Born in 1936, a decade before Roger, Louis "Bob" Trinchero dresses more like the local hardware store owner than the CEO of a multi-million-case winery. Amiable, amusing, and self-assured, he married his high school sweetheart, follows the Pritikin diet religiously, and anchors the family's stability. Like the middle-aged Mario, Bob sports a round, Charlie Brown head, thinning hair, and a friendly grin that comes easily. Bob says he shaves his father's face every morning. "I look so much like my dad. We have the same basketball kind of head," Bob says with characteristic humor. His father and uncle taught him how to make wine, but it was Bob who stumbled on the fortuitous accident, the creation of Sutter Home White Zinfandel, that would ultimately transform the family's mom-and-pop operation into one of the world's largest wineries.

Vera Trinchero Torres' soft complexion and poise belie an inner strength that has helped her overcome a history of hardships. The only daughter in this intensely Italian family, Vera was also the only sibling to work most of her life outside the struggling family business. "They couldn't afford to pay me," she says. Two years younger than her brother Bob, Vera sustained and overcame serious health problems: bypass surgery, breast cancer, nerve damage in her wrist, and other maladies. Her once dark locks, now streaked with silver, curl gently around her head. She is, like her brother Bob, often described as "quite a character," due to her kindness and unbridled generosity melded with a sharp but restrained feistiness. Long divorced, she is the only sibling whose children, Tony and Bobby Torres, chose careers in the family business.

As dissimilar as Roger, Bob, and Vera first appear, they share the same intense, powerful eyes: dark, large, round, and deep. They radiate confidence, sincerity, conviction, and compassion. Their eyes are so distinctive that even in photographs they attract the viewer's interest over all other details, like the eyes in Byzantine portraits of the ancient Roman Empire.

If it's true that you can tell something about a people's character by looking in their eyes, then the Trincheros' eyes reveal volumes about themselves—all positive, all strong, and all as bewitching as their father Mario's eyes. This is their story.

HEADING WEST

December 5, 1948, was a rainy, foggy day in northern California. After a three-day, cross-country train ride from New York City, Mary Trinchero and her three children— Bob, 12, Vera, 10, and Roger, 2—arrived at the Oakland train depot. Mary's husband, Mario, who had come West several months earlier, was there to greet them, and the family drove two and a half hours to the small town of St. Helena in Napa Valley to begin their new lives as vintners at Sutter Home Winery.

"We pulled into the winery, which was a dilapidated old barn that hadn't operated since before Prohibition," Bob Trinchero remembers. "It had been abandoned and was waist high in weeds in the front, with dirt floors and no electricity. My mother started to cry. We came from mid-town Manhattan, where we had a pretty nice lifestyle, so we couldn't understand why my dad would bring us to a place like this."

Trading a cozy lifestyle in New York for an unknown future in a place as far across the nation as you could get to launch a new career in the then-tiny California wine business may not seem that odd to many Americans. After all, entrepreneurship weaves throughout the fabric of our nation's history. But Mario Trinchero, who turned 50 his first year at the winery, was no longer a young man. His wife, Mary, was 37. She grew up in an Italian convent after her parents died and worked in a sweater factory in New York before marrying Mario. She raised their three young children well, and, while no stranger to work, had no idea the future for which she and the family left New York would be so drastically different.

"Why didn't you tell me it was going to be like this?" Mary asked Mario. "Because," Bob recalls his father saying, "if I had, you would never have come." Her three children agree—she wouldn't have.

That winter and the following spring were difficult seasons for the new arrivals to the valley. While Mario and his brother John converted an old, two-story barn on the winery property into living quarters, the Trincheros lived for seven months in a small, unheated motel cabin with no indoor bathroom. Like their mother, the children struggled to adjust from the sophistication of New York City to the rural simplicity of St. Helena.

Napa Valley was a far different place in 1948 than it is today. It was completely rural, with more acres of prunes and walnuts than grapes, and a sizable amount of land was given over to tomato farming and cattle grazing. There were only a handful of wineries.

"I remember as a boy making spare money picking walnuts and prunes, and I remember the prune dehydrator south of town where Bob worked when he was in high school," Roger says. "The lifestyle then was a lot slower and, unlike today, there was no tourism. Napa Valley was definitely off the beaten path."

That description probably explains why, after years amid the excitement and bustle of midtown Manhattan, Mary Trinchero began crying when she first saw Sutter Home. "Actually" recalls Bob, "she cried for three months."

ADJUSTMENT

The Trinchero children did not cry as their mother had, but they were equally befuddled. "I couldn't believe that when you picked up the phone, you got an operator who completed your call," Vera says. "We had direct dialing in Manhattan! And the kids in my class thought I was from Europe because they couldn't understand my New York accent."

If the local kids thought the Trinchero children were odd, Bob, Vera, and Roger were even more stunned by their surroundings. "Even before seeing Dad," Bob recalls, "as we pulled into the station, I thought, 'We're in the wilderness.' I thought my dad had kinda lost it. I kept wondering what was going on. I couldn't put it together.

"Then, when we got off the train and I saw my dad standing there in a short-sleeved shirt and Levi's," recalls Bob, "I burst out laughing. I thought it was a joke. I'd never seen my dad wear anything like that. Back in New York, my father wore three-piece suits, a tie, a nice hat, an overcoat, sometimes an ascot. He used to be a sharp dresser. A couple of times, we visited him where he

worked and he wore a tuxedo with tails. He was a bartender, but I mean the high-end type of bartender. I'd
always seen him dressed up, always impeccably dressed.
Now I saw him in a short-sleeved shirt, which I'd never
seen him in before in my life, and—a pair of Levi's jeans!"
Bob scrunches his face in amazement, eyes wide and glassy,
but speaks somberly. "What was this?! was my reaction. I
started to laugh, a nervous laughter. It was like they took
my whole world and completely turned it upside down. It
was weird."

Bob's early weeks in St. Helena caused the family even
more concern. "I kept hearing this buzzing sound in my
ears, a whining all the time," he recalls. "So they took me
to the doctor, who asked where we lived beforehand. We
came from New York, a big city, and we were on 66th
Street. If you know 66th Street on the West Side, it's one
of the few two-way streets, and it goes across Central Park.
All night long there's traffic noise. Then you have the St.
Nicholas arena, which was right across the street from us,
where they had all the fights and wrestling. Noise all the
time. So now, it's quiet in St. Helena. There's no noise
whatsoever. Except this constant whining sound in my
head. Apparently, the pastoral quietness and lack of traffic
in St. Helena was so foreign, I couldn't take it. The doctor
said it would go away, and sure enough, a couple weeks
later it was gone."

Life in California took a real adjustment. "I don't
remember my exact feelings at first, but I remember being
apprehensive, especially when I went to school. I mean here
I was dressed for school: slacks, white shirt, tie. Whooee!"
Bob turns his head slowly and makes a noise that resembles
a noooo and a wooo. "A good idea? I don't think so! When
I came home that first school day, I said, 'Ma, you gotta buy
me a pair of these things called blue jeans—which is what

they called them back then. In New York, the family said 'dungarees.' So she went down to Goodman's here in town and bought me a pair. Of course, back then, they were really more like canvas. They stood up on their own, and when they'd get wet, your legs and thighs would turn blue. Whew! That was terrible."

But the most drastic change was the place where the Trincheros first lived. The El Bonita Motel, situated on the main highway just south of the town of St. Helena, is today a contemporary, upscale motel, hip and trendy in a retro-deco sort of way. Rooms go from $135 to nearly $300 a night for poolside suites. El Bonita's neon sign beckons valley tourists, and the outside of the place is painted a crisp, eye-catching pink. But in the 1940s, the El Bonita was a run-down, rustic set of cabins with few amenities. Yet it was walking distance to the Sutter Home Winery, and really the only place available for the Trincheros to stay.

"We stayed at the El Bonita all winter, spring, and half the summer," recalls Vera. "There was no indoor plumbing, so we had to carry our chamber pots out in the morning. The shower was communal. Worst of all, there was no heat. We had a small electric heater, but the owner at that time wouldn't let us use it, because he said it cost him an additional $50 a month in electricity. We lived in two rooms, with a room that was actually an enclosed porch. In cold weather, the walls would sweat."

With every rag used to wipe down the cold, clammy, sweating walls of their El Bonita lodgings, Mary's depression grew worse. The kids had never seen her so upset, especially for so long. Not that she didn't have good reason to cry. Mary had been happy in New York. She had no desire to change her life. But if it was going to be different, she dreamed that at least it would be better. This most certainly was not.

Everyone seemed to miss the lifestyle they enjoyed in New York. Everyone, that is, except little Roger and his father Mario.

NEW YORK DAYS

Mario shooed his wife and their three kids out the door. "*Ecco la!* That's it, go play in the park, run in the sunshine. I'll see you tonight."

It was Monday, and Mario dressed casually in comfortable slacks and a white shirt. No one but his family ever saw him in such plain clothes. For the rest of New York, Mario wore dapper three-piece suits, or even a tux and tails, and appeared just as classy as the patrons he served at the Barbizon Plaza, Waldorf-Astoria, or other high-society New York hotels of the time.

Mario was not a wealthy man, but the $250 a week he earned in the 1940s as a waiter or bartender was enough for his family to live comfortably, even in New York. "We lived in a large, well-kept brownstone apartment on West 66th Street, right smack in the middle of Manhattan, just a block away from Central Park West," recalls Vera.

"Every Monday, Dad sent Mom and us kids off to Central Park. Even on his day off, he took care of all of us. Dad cleaned the entire apartment and had a nice hot dinner waiting for us when we came back." Those Monday dinners were important to the Trincheros. They were among the few times the kids saw their father. "He worked as a bartender at night and would come home at four in the morning. When I got up to go to my school, P.S. 94 at West 68th and Amsterdam," recalls Bob, "Dad slept, and when I came home from school he had already gone to work."

No one knows for sure why Mario decided to gamble on a vintner's life. But for a man devoted to family and family values, perhaps the night jobs that kept him from Mary and the kids contributed to his decision. Vera thinks a combination of factors led to his move West. "Basically he was tired of being a bartender. He was afraid of becoming an alcoholic, because everyone wants to buy the bartender a drink, plus the fact that his mother died. If his mother hadn't died the year before, he would not have moved. He was very, very close to Nonna. So when brother John called him to come out here, he said, yeah, I'm gonna be my own boss again. And that's how it started."

Prior to the move, Mario never displayed any desire to leave New York, change his career, or make wine. "Dad was a happy man, a prankster. He was an adventurer, a partier—he always loved a good time," describes Bob.

"He married my mother when he was 36 and she was 24, there's 12 years difference between them. Other than his day off, the only time we saw him was on weekends, when it was party time at the house. People would show up and we'd have this five- to six-hour lunch-dinner combination."

"Mario was the main cook," remembers Vera. His family ran their own restaurant in Italy, opening another restaurant in New Jersey after they arrived in the United States. "So he grew up with cooking, and he was a great cook. The only thing he refused to do all his life was wash the dishes. At family get-togethers, Dad did the turkey or the ham, the hors d'oeuvres, the entrée, and mixed the cocktails. He did all types of recipes. Mom did the vegetables and side dishes, and she was the pasta cooker. She made the raviolis from scratch, which was a lot of work. I used to help. It was fun on a rainy Sunday, when there was nothing to do outside. Meals were always a community effort."

Bob recalls those days fondly, when Mario cooked and the rest of his family joined him. "The kids would eat and leave, but the parents, they'd fight World War I on the tablecloth with pens and pencils. Once, my Aunt Vera, my mother's oldest sister, brought her second husband over. The adults swapped war stories, going, 'We were here, in this place . . . and then we went there . . .' and so on. My aunt's husband was new to the family, so his stories were also new—quite a bonus, since everyone else rehashed the same stories over and over again for years. All of a sudden, they realized there was a possibility that this guy could have dropped bombs on my father, because he had been a bombardier for the Germans. He was from the Italian-Austrian border, which the Austrians owned at the time, so he fought for the Germans, the *tedeschi*." With a boyish laugh, Bob adds, "It was really strange. They all looked at each other and said 'You dropped bombs *where?*' "

Life in New York was full of good times, close relatives, festive food, and Italian camaraderie. After the move to California, many years passed before the Trincheros experienced the same degree of comfort and relaxed enjoyment.

2

Vino Vecchio

Although Mario never expressed any desire to get involved in the California wine business, wine was part of his heritage, both as an Italian and through his family history. The Trinchero family's participation in the California wine business dates to 1948, but their involvement in wine goes back much further—to the nineteenth century in their Italian homeland.

The Trincheros came from Asti, in Italy's northwest province of Piemonte, a center of fine wine making and home to two of Italy's most famous wines, Barolo and Barbaresco, both produced from the Nebbiolo grape. The area is also known for its fine Barberas, and a branch of the family still resides in Piemonte and remains a leading producer.

Mario Trinchero's father, Luigi, owned a vineyard in the Asti area that twice was destroyed by hail. As Bob explains, "You know, in Italy they have hailstones the size of baseballs. I can't figure that! And they still have them today: A hailstorm in 2002 severely damaged the Barolo and Barbaresco vineyards. My grandfather in Italy suffered two years of these devastating hailstones. They were young

13

vines, and the hail just destroyed them. He replanted them, and they were destroyed again. So he said, 'That's it. *Basta!*' And in 1901 he came here."

Two years after Mario's birth, Luigi ventured to the United States alone to earn money for his family, which, in addition to his wife, Luigia, and son Mario, included sons John, Julio, and Marino, and daughters Dina and Diana.

After working for five years in Maine as a lumberjack and sending money home regularly, Luigi returned to Italy. "In 1906," Bob recounts, "he came home, took the family off the farm, and relocated to Savona, a small seaport north of Genoa. They had a two-story place by the harbor, with a winery downstairs. Upstairs was a restaurant, a lunch-room catering to the longshoremen. My grandmother and the kids fixed the lunches, and my grandfather and his old-est son John made the wine in the basement, then took it to all the accounts. That's how John, who was the first Trinchero to get involved in Sutter Home Winery, learned to make wine."

In 1915, at the age of 16, Mario Trinchero was con-scripted into the Italian army, as his older brother John had been in 1912. While John spent six years fighting in Abyssinia (now Ethiopia), Mario survived World War I in Europe. After the war, Mario, Marino, and Dina settled in Lyons, France.

In 1919, the Volstead Act ushered in Prohibition. The same year, Mario's other sister, Diana, moved to New York City, where she, too, married an Italian, whom the family referred to as "the Little Gangster." The couple opened a speakeasy in Manhattan, which became so successful it allowed Diana to bring virtually her entire family to the United States during the early 1920s. Dina was the only one to remain in France, by choice. Mario and his brother Marino arrived on U.S. shores in 1923.

THE LITTLE GANGSTER

"I don't know why Aunt Diana came to the United States; I never found out," says Bob. "But once she was here, she got tied up with this guy, the Little Gangster. That's what they called him, too, the Little Gangster. My mother told me his name once, but no one called him that, whatever it was. Together, Diana and the Little Gangster operated a speakeasy, and she slowly brought everyone in the family over, including my grandfather, grandmother, and her brothers. In 1923, Mario and his youngest brother Marino (who passed away in 2002 at age 90) were the last ones to come to the United States. So they were all together again, in the United States, running this speakeasy. Then she got a divorce from the gangster—I heard it was because he was playing around." (Ironically, Diana would later remarry, this time not to a crook, but to a retired cop; he came complete with a retired police dog, a German shepherd named Prince who became one of Vera's favorite pets.)

Running a speakeasy in the Roaring Twenties may sound glamorous to some, or shocking to the more prudish. But some of today's leading wine families survived Prohibition by operating speakeasies or making the wine that was served in them. Some, like Cesare Mondavi, father of Robert and Peter Mondavi, earned a tidy living by buying and selling the California grapes that other Italians, from coast to coast, crushed into their homemade wine. The contacts Cesare made in the grape-shipping business later became the distributors of the wines he made after the repeal of Prohibition in 1933.

While the Trincheros operated the Little Gangster's establishment on the East Coast, their fellow countrymen Giuseppe and Michelo ("Mike") Gallo were hopscotching the San Francisco Bay Area, running one of the West Coast's most successful bootleg operations. The Gallos hauled wine and distilled spirits, selling to whomever would buy them—including undercover agents. Mike, the leader in the business and described by the Feds as an "Oakland rum runner," was ultimately jailed for bootlegging. Giuseppe fell into severe debt during Mike's incarceration, then lost his remaining savings in the stock market Crash of 1929. Giuseppe's sons, Ernest and Julio, would later convert the family business into the largest wine company in the world.

PROHIBITION TO PARADISE

The Trincheros' Prohibition experiences weren't nearly as dark as those of many other early winemakers. In fact, they were quite positive. In the latter part of the decade, the family moved to Lake George in upstate New York, where they opened a restaurant-speakeasy called the Paradise Inn. With its huge garden, lush with trees and grassy lawns, the Paradise Inn became a weekend destination spot for New Yorkers wishing to imbibe peacefully in the verdant countryside.

As they had in Italy, father Luigi and his son John made wine at the Paradise Inn, including sparkling wine. "My dad also helped make wine, but mostly he was the delivery guy," explains Bob. Bob's Uncle Julio was a skilled mechanic, so he kept the car in good running condition, servicing it between the alcohol runs from New York to New Jersey. "Dad had a Dodge with a false floor to hide the wine. He got caught once, though, and they took all of his stuff away from him. But he made $500 a week during Prohibition. Now that was really good! A lot better than bartending.

"I once asked him, didn't you get in trouble with the Mafia? He said no. As a matter of fact, they sold to the mob. My grandfather was a champagne maker, and he used to sell sparkling wine to organized crime members for their own enjoyment. For a family to make and sell wine caused no problems with the Mafia. They were after the liquor and the beer business. For them, everybody could make wine. After all, wine was part of the heritage."

The Volstead Act

Congress ratified the Eighteenth Amendment prohibiting the commercial sale of any intoxicating liquor in 1917, but it would not become effective until January 16, 1920. Under pressure to curtail alcohol consumption sooner, Congress passed the Volstead Act, which implemented the enforcement of the Prohibition amendment and was effective immediately, on October 28, 1919. However, the Volstead Act contained a loophole that permitted heads of households to make up to 200 gallons of wine per year. Volstead also permitted medicinal wine and sacramental wine. Thus, a few wineries skated through this period by making wines for consecration.

The loophole sustained California grape growers through Prohibition, because grapes skyrocketed in demand. Many people switched from beer and hard alcohol and drank more wine than ever before. Before the war, Americans consumed an estimated 53 million gallons of wine annually. In 1928, the federal government estimated that Americans drank 154 million gallons. Growers shipped California grapes across the nation, and home winemakers and bootleggers eagerly turned them into wine.

Speakeasies Flourish

The pre-Prohibition saloon morphed into the speakeasy, but instead of neon lights and big street signs, speakeasies appeared clandestinely in back rooms, basements, office buildings, or anyplace that allowed for a less public, though accessible, entryway. Speakeasies populated big cities coast to coast, and San Francisco was as notorious for its speakeasies as New York. Cops raided the speakeasies on a regular basis, but rarely closed them down permanently. The triangular-shaped Hotel d'Oloron off Columbus Avenue in San Francisco typified the process. Every time the Feds raided the hotel and its bootleg bar, they asked the judge to shut down the premises at the hotel's street address. The hotel owner simply called out the carpenters to cut open a new doorway to the alley, and a new address and business were born. By the time Prohibition was repealed, a string of doors made the place so legendary, it became a favorite haunt of the press, who admired the owner's chutzpah (Flamm 1999).

Although speakeasies were technically illegal, they flourished as part of the "noble" but failed experiment of Prohibition. Even in Italian neighborhoods, small cafés, without being as elaborate as speakeasies, served wine to their patrons—not in wine glasses but in coffee cups, lest a federal agent or constable should wander in.

According to Vera, her mother told her that, at that time in New Jersey, everyone had cellars. "The families would live in the upstairs part of the house and rent the cellars out to bootleggers to make their gin, or whatever. So the speakeasy business wasn't scorned or even that unusual. It was just a cooperative—no one thought anything about it."

Prohibition Fails

In 1925, over 100,000 speakeasies did business in New York City alone. Rochester, New York, close to the Canadian border, became a destination for smugglers and home to more than twice as many speakeasies as the entire number of saloons shuttered by Prohibition.

Though intended to reduce crime and corruption, Prohibition had the opposite effect. Bootleggers grew rich running spirits from overseas or Canada, or distilling the hooch themselves. Competing mobsters and organized crime gangs took the illegal alcohol business and its gushing profits seriously. Once they got hold of it, they weren't about to let go.

Violent crime skyrocketed, especially in large cities. New York's homicide rate nearly doubled compared to what it had been prior to Prohibition. Collectively, major crimes—including homicide, burglary, and assault—increased 24 percent between 1920 and 1924 alone. Prohibition effectively created a black market so profitable that crime became organized, violent, and unrelenting. Some crimes decreased, but they were mainly victimless acts like swearing and vagrancy.

When Prohibition ended in 1933, the Paradise Inn closed and the Trinchero family split up. John found a wine-making job in Paterson, New Jersey, and Mario moved back to New York City, where he worked as a waiter and bartender.

MARIO AND MARY, PLUS THREE

In 1935, Mario met and married Mary Beda, who was born in Pittsburgh in 1911 and had moved to Italy with her mother and sisters in 1914. After their parents died when Mary was 10, she and her sisters lived in a convent boarding school in Piemonte, under the supervision of their aunts and uncles, until 1931. In 1932, Mary returned to

Pittsburgh, then moved to Manhattan, where she worked in a sweater factory and met Mario.

In 1936, the couple had their first child, Louis, whose name was an English translation of Luigi. But Mary never liked the name Louis, so she called him "Bobby," and the nickname stuck. (Today, he is still referred to as Louis "Bob" Trinchero.) Daughter Vera and son Roger followed, each retaining their baptized names. Perhaps Mario yielded more flexibly to Mary's wishes when naming the younger children.

Despite the difference in ages—Bob is two years older than Vera and ten years older than Roger—the siblings have stayed remarkably close. "Our birthdays—Bob's, Roger's, and mine—all fall within the same week," notes Vera, suggesting that this may have reinforced in some unspoken way their connection to each other as siblings rather than rivals. "We were born in different years, of course, but all within the same calendar week." As Bob says with a sparkle, "My parents must have had a special time of year."

The family moved into a large brownstone on West 66th Street in midtown Manhattan. Life was good. Despite Mario's night hours working as a bartender, the family still placed tremendous importance on being together, not just the parents and kids, but aunts, uncles, in-laws, and, most important, Nonna, Mario's mother, who lived with his sister, Diana, in New Jersey. "Dad was very, very close to his mom. They were a hugely close family, all of them," recalls Vera.

As in all good Italian homes, wine flowed freely and was never considered anything but a regular beverage. Everyone, from the oldest to the youngest, accepted wine as part of the family's daily routine.

Bob speaks fondly of those times with his grandmother, whom he describes as "the sweetest woman you could ever imagine." Because of her, he first found pleasure in a wine's taste. Many wine drinkers today say they learned to enjoy wine when they tasted Sutter Home White Zinfandel, because it is slightly sweet. Ironically, it was Nonna's special wine concoction that had the same impact on Bob Trinchero.

"I don't recall the first time I sipped wine, but I remember vividly the first time I started to enjoy it," says Bob. "Nonna, my grandmother, always thought that red wine was too strong. First of all, you didn't drink white wine back then. Nobody drank white wine. I *never* saw a bottle of white wine on our table in New York. It was always a jug of Fior d'Italia, by the gallon. It was poured in a tumbler. Well, my grandmother thought it was too strong for her, so she mixed it half and half with 7-Up. That has to be the first wine cooler that I've ever heard of. This was around 1945, when I was just eight or nine years old. Well, I tried it and I *loved* it. The drink was sweet, and, you know, a bit carbonated. So my parents would pour about 25 percent red wine and 75 percent 7-Up in a cup for me. And that's what I wanted. Every time I'd sit down at the table, that's what I wanted. I *really* enjoyed it. And actually, if you've never tasted it, the mix makes a dynamite cocktail. As far as drinking wine straight, I never really cared for it, at least not until I got much older. But as a kid, I did take it with 7-Up."

During this period, Mario earned a good living working as a bartender in upscale midtown hotels and restaurants. His brother John, however, abandoned his job in New Jersey for the allure of California.

In 1945, John visited the Golden State to purchase bulk wine for his employer, the Italian-French Winery. Smitten by bucolic Napa Valley, he moved there the following year and persuaded an East Coast friend, Louis Carlesimo, to help him purchase an old abandoned winery called Sutter Home, on Highway 29 south of the small town of St. Helena. Escrow closed in January 1947.

Carlesimo, who had remained in New York, soon abandoned the project. John Trinchero realized he couldn't go it alone in California and importuned his brother Mario to move to St. Helena to become his partner at Sutter Home.

In the summer of 1948, Mario finally relented. He was 49 years old, with a wife and three children, and enjoyed a comfortable middle-class existence in the most exciting city on earth.

But a new life beckoned.

3

Sutter Home

The saga of Sutter Home Winery, prior to the Trincheros' purchase of it, embodies the early history of Napa Valley, a wine industry devastated by the 1906 San Francisco earthquake and fire, the banking panic of 1907 (in which wine-drinking foreigners left the country in search of jobs), a killer frost in 1916, and Prohibition, the final blow that shattered the original Sutter Home's wine production.

The winery that the Trinchero family began reviving in 1948, although dormant for 30 years following the advent of Prohibition in 1918, was one of Napa's oldest. Established in 1874 by a Swiss-German immigrant named John Thomann, it prospered during the final quarter of the nineteenth century.

GOLD RUSH TO GRAPE CRUSH

John Thomann, a stocky and sturdy young man, sporting a beard right off of a Smith Brothers cough drop logo, eagerly anticipated each letter he received from his uncle, Henry Thomann.

Henry emigrated from Switzerland and settled in St. Louis, but he kept in touch with his young nephew. A born adventurer, Henry felt the call of the American West and set out in 1845 for California, just a year before the Donner Party attempted their fatal journey across the same terrain.

California was the ideal place for Henry's adventurous spirit. In 1846, he served with General M. G. Vallejo during the Bear Flag Rebellion, which took place in Sonoma County, Napa's neighbor. Son of a Spanish officer, Vallejo was a highly educated man who at one time owned large tracts of northern California territory, including much of what is now Marin, Sonoma, Napa, and Solano Counties. Though Vallejo was a Mexican commander, he personally supported the idea of an independent and self-governing Republic of California, which was the goal of the Bear Flag Rebellion. But to U.S. Captain John Fremont, an influential leader at the time, Vallejo represented Mexico, and Fremont ordered him and his family arrested.

Though the Bear Flag flew over the newly proclaimed "Republic of California" for less than 60 days, after the revolt Mexico ceded all of California and the Southwest to the United States in 1848—the same year that gold was discovered in a California sawmill owned by Captain John Sutter and a century before Mario Trinchero set down stakes in California.

John Sutter, a Swiss émigré, wanted to establish a "New Helvetia" in the New World. In the early 1840s in the Sacramento Valley, his dream came true. This particular Sutter has no relation to the present Sutter Home Winery, but he did impact the lives of Henry Thomann and, ultimately, Henry's nephew John Thomann.

Fremont sent the Vallejos to Sutter's Fort, as John Sutter's pioneering enclave was christened. At the same time, Henry Thomann also arrived at Sutter's Fort, where he became acquainted with John Sutter, a relationship that led to a future in grapes.

Besides building his fort into a European community and traveler's stop, Sutter learned how to farm. He recruited workers for his settlement from all parts of Mexico's California territory, the United States, Switzerland, and Germany. Henry, a natural-born Swiss like Sutter, and with experience of the American West, was especially welcome at Sutter's Fort. Before long, Henry worked for Sutter and eventually earned enough money to purchase land in Sacramento. Within a few seasons, he tilled the land into a thriving vineyard and was on his way to becoming a successful winemaker.

Perhaps John Sutter should have followed Henry Thomann's lead and pursued the wine business, for the discovery of gold at Sutter's Mill eventually led to his complete ruin. The gold rush started out with great promise, as Sutter describes in a letter to Henry Thomann in 1848: "Gold is now found twenty miles from here and travels up to the sawmill in a width of twenty to thirty miles and about forty miles in length; that is, as far as we have traced it. . . ." (Lewis 1966).

The gold rush, though it sounds glamorous, in truth brought a wave of lawlessness to Sutter's civilized fort. Sutter was known for his generosity, and almost everyone who passed through took advantage of it, to his detriment. Eventually, Sutter suffered both spiritual and financial bankruptcy. Elderly and in poor health, he and his wife boarded a steamer for the East Coast in 1865 and never returned to the West. He died in 1880—about the time many Californians were about to make their first fortune from wine, the liquid gold of the vine.

Thomann's Liquid Gold

While Sutter fell deep into debt, Henry Thomann's bountiful vineyards inspired his nephew, John, to leave Switzerland in 1853 and join him in Sacramento. After working for his uncle until Henry's death in 1870, John ran the family business for four years before striking out on his own.

In 1874, he moved to Napa Valley and established the John Thomann Winery and Distillery just south of St. Helena. Thomann owned 45 acres of grapes on Howell Mountain east of the valley floor (today renowned for its Zinfandel and Cabernet vines) and prided himself on using only mountain-grown grapes for his wines. Thomann eschewed the popular Mission grape, as well as other varieties predominant in the valley, which he considered inferior material for fine wine, although suitable for his daily production of 800 gallons of brandy.

Thomann's Napa Valley venture proved successful, perhaps setting the stage for what would occur nearly a century later. In his first year, he produced 40,000 gallons of wine. By the early 1880s, Thomann's annual production reached an impressive 200,000 gallons (roughly 83,000 cases), all in the building that today houses the Trinchero family's Sutter Home Visitors Center. By contrast, 100 years later, the Trincheros' production of Sutter Home White Zinfandel leaped from 25,000 cases in 1981 to a whopping 1.5 million cases in 1986.

Boom to Bust

The 1880s ushered in California's first wine boom, and John Thomann joined other immigrant luminaries, such as

Charles Krug, Jacob Beringer, and Jacob Schram, as leaders of Napa Valley's burgeoning wine industry and as pillars of the community. (Thomann served on the school board and as a county supervisor.)

The northern California wine industry in the nineteenth century was organized very differently than it is today. Rarely did wineries age, bottle, or distribute their own wines. Rather, those functions occurred in numerous wine cellars in San Francisco, from which finished wines were distributed by rail or boat to markets across the United States. A winery's cellar was empty long before the next vintage arrived.

In the early 1880s, California was known among fine-wine enthusiasts primarily for Riesling and Zinfandel wines (the latter often called "Claret" in emulation of French Bordeaux), as well as for fortified wines such as port and sherry. Napa Valley, along with the Valley of the Moon in Sonoma (where writer Jack London lived), enjoyed the greatest reputation for quality. Grape and wine prices rose steadily each year.

Reflecting his prosperity, John Thomann, in 1884, constructed a grandiose Victorian home adjacent to the winery for his wife and four daughters. The family inhabited it until 1900, when Thomann died unexpectedly during a visit to Switzerland. With no interest in the wine industry, Thomann's children suspended production and gradually sold off the winery's equipment. They also sold their furniture and eventually abandoned the grand house along with the winery.

In 1906 another Swiss family, the Leuenbergers, purchased the once-thriving estate at a sheriff's sale for $10 in gold. The Leuenbergers initiated the next phase in the winery's history.

MUST TO DUST

Caroline and Emil Leuenberger arrived in the United States from Switzerland in the mid-1880s. Caroline's father, John A. Sutter (no relation to John Sutter, the pioneer explorer and discoverer of gold), was a Bay Area businessman and former sea captain. Emil Leuenberger first worked as a farmer and then a bookkeeper. In 1890 his wife and he purchased 80 acres of land on the lower slopes of Howell Mountain and founded a winery called Sutter Home, named in honor of Caroline's father.

In 1895, the Leuenbergers established a wine and spirits firm called the Sutter Home Winery and Distillery Company on Folsom Street in San Francisco, to which they shipped Sutter Home wines for blending, aging, bottling, and distribution. For the next decade, the company prospered.

Disaster upon Disaster

On April 18, 1906, the great San Francisco earthquake and fire struck. The area south of Market Street, which housed most of the industry's great wine cellars, was hit hardest, and up to 15 million gallons of wine were destroyed.

The Leuenbergers, like many others, lost everything. In the aftermath of the disaster, many wine businesses relocated to areas outside of the city deemed to be safer, where they unified production, aging, storage, and shipping activities under a single roof. While searching for a facility, the Leuenbergers discovered the large, abandoned Thomann Winery, which happened to have its own railroad spur as well as a spacious home.

After purchasing the Thomann Winery in 1906, the Leuenbergers renamed it Sutter Home (dubbing Thomann's

Victorian home Chalet Bernensis, after the Swiss canton of Bern, where the Leuenbergers were born) and subsequently sold their Howell Mountain winery.

The Leuenbergers painted the words "SUTTER HOME WINERY" in letters the size of horses across the roof of the winery, which was visible, because of its angle, not just from the air but also to drivers passing along the road. Had the Leuenbergers not done that, Mario and John might have named their winery Trinchero Family Estates in 1948, rather than waiting until 1999 to do so. But in 1948 the words "SUTTER HOME WINERY" were still hugely tattooed on the building. To call the winery anything else would have been confusing. John and Mario looked at the roof and knew full well that the cost of paint was not in their budget. So they agreed: The name would stay. After all, it was professionally painted and reflected a sense of heritage and quality. At the time, the Trincheros were not concerned that their wines didn't bear the family name. They just wanted their wines to sell.

Back in 1906, the Leuenbergers entrusted wine making at Sutter Home to one of Caroline Leuenberger's brothers, Albert Sutter. They maintained residence in San Francisco, where Caroline was an eminent modiste (dress designer) catering to the city's wealthy matrons. She employed 35 people in her Post Street shop and traveled each spring and autumn to France to study the latest Parisian fashions. Although the Leuenbergers spent weekends and summers in St. Helena, they didn't take up permanent residence at Chalet Bernensis until 1914.

The Leuenbergers' tenure at their new facility was troubled from the beginning. The panic of 1907, which led to the near-collapse of the American banking industry, caused a prolonged economic depression. Over 100,000 wine-loving foreigners of southern European descent left the depleted U.S. job market to return home, resulting in a loss of 2.5 million gallons in annual wine consumption.

In 1908, Sutter Home's wine production fell to 45,000 gallons, a sizable drop from the 200,000 gallons in 1900, when Thomann died. In 1909, no wine at all was made, although the winery continued its distillery operations. That same year, price wars erupted between large and small wine producers, and wholesale wine prices plummeted from 25 to 15 cents per gallon, while grape prices dropped from an average of $20 per ton to just $10 per ton. As a result, by 1912, California's wine grape acreage had declined by 30 percent.

The War on Wine

In 1914, the situation improved. Sutter Home resumed purchasing grapes and made 60,000 gallons of wine. However, that year, to finance the nascent war effort, the federal government adopted a six-cent per gallon tax on wine. Concomitantly, a proposition calling for a prohibition on the sale, distribution, and consumption of alcoholic beverages appeared on the California state ballot. Although it lost, vintners had a presentiment of the nightmare to come.

The Leuenbergers were in Europe when World War I broke out. On their return, they moved into Chalet Bernensis while storm clouds gathered. One by one, states across the country enacted some form of antialcohol legislation. Even the *St. Helena Star,* a mouthpiece for the local wine industry, changed the name of a regular column from "Wines and Vines Notes" to "Vineyard, Orchard and Farms" and shifted coverage from wine to the local tree fruit and animal farming industries.

The war brought heavy taxes and a growing prohibitionist sentiment. The production of more highly taxed fortified wines dropped from 20 million gallons in 1913 to less than 3 million gallons in 1914, and table wine production declined 60 percent. In 1916, Napa suffered a further blow from a killing frost, which cut the year's grape crop in half.

These problems were further exacerbated by conflicts between growers and producers. Growers supported proposed state legislation prohibiting the sale of hard liquor, believing it would boost wine sales in restaurants and package shops. But vintners opposed the law, correctly fearing it would move California one step closer to a complete ban on alcoholic beverages.

The entry of America into the war in 1917 accelerated the alcohol surge. Prohibitionists joined forces with patriotic groups to promote legislation banning the conversion of "foodstuffs" into alcohol. The fact that grapes were different in this regard from the wheat, barley, and rice used to make beer and distilled spirits was conveniently ignored.

In August 1918, the Wartime Agricultural Act (WAA) passed, which banned the sale of all alcoholic beverages until American armed forces were demobilized. By this time, 75 percent of the states in the union had passed "dry" legislation. Even though the war ended before the WAA was enacted, the courts let it stand on the basis that a formal peace treaty had yet to be signed. By that time, at the Treaty of Versailles, the Eighteenth Amendment to the Constitution, installing Prohibition, had been ratified. The American wine industry was dead.

Prohibition ended the wine-making career of the Leuenberger family. Like most other Napa Valley wineries, Sutter Home was dormant during Prohibition, which ended in 1933. By then, the Leuenbergers were in their seventies and disinterested in reviving the winery.

It remained shuttered until 1947, when the Trinchero

family acquired it. At that time, Caroline Leuenberger still resided in the nineteenth century Victorian mansion constructed by John Thomann. (Her husband, Emil, had died in 1936.) On her death in 1949, the mansion passed to her nephew, Louis Sutter, chairman of the Crocker-Anglo Bank, who put it up for sale for $12,000. Because the Trincheros could not afford to purchase it, the house passed through several hands, becoming, at various times, an antique shop and a bed-and-breakfast inn. It was not until 1986, after White Zinfandel became a commercial success, that the Trincheros finally acquired the Victorian and reunited the historic wine estate.

THE LOOPHOLE

Ironically, although Prohibition destroyed the California wine industry, it actually bolstered the state's grape industry because, in a loophole engineered by New York City mayor Fiorello La Guardia, households were allowed to make up to 200 gallons of wine each year. Thus, the market for California grapes during Prohibition was actually greater than in the years immediately preceding it. Trains loaded with California grapes headed out to all parts of the United States, especially those destined for New York, Chicago, and wherever Italian neighborhoods thrived.

"Every harvest, the trains from California would arrive," Bob Trinchero explains. "The stations were crowded. People would head to the train depots where they'd fill up their trucks with the boxes of grapes. There were a series of stores there, too, where you could buy your labels and your bottles and your corks, all the equipment for making wine. Remember that a head of household could produce up to

200 gallons of wine per year, and believe me, a lot of it was going on. So they'd buy their grapes and all their supplies, and they'd go home to their basements or other hidden places and start making it. The law was pretty sexist back then, too. They did not consider a woman to be a head of household. They finally changed the wording. Now, any adult can make 200 gallons. But back then, it meant men only." Yet, no matter what the law stated, the homemade wine business was a family affair, and every member from youngsters to grandparents participated.

Because much of the grape crop during this period shipped in unrefrigerated railroad cars to home winemakers on the East Coast, rugged, thick-skinned varieties like Carignane and Alicante Bouschet were cultivated, and higher-quality but more fragile varieties were ripped out. When commercial wine making resumed in the mid-1930s, the prevalence of these hardy but pedestrian reds retarded the industry's ability to rehabilitate itself quickly.

Also, the Prohibition years literally altered the north coast landscape, especially in Napa Valley, where many grape growers switched to growing prunes, later to be joined by thousands of acres of walnuts and cattle.

After the repeal of Prohibition many rushed to join the renascent wine industry. Unfortunately, few experienced winemakers remained, and the newcomers had more energy and enthusiasm than expertise, resulting in a large quantity of inferior wine. Some bottles, still fermenting, even exploded on store shelves. Further, Americans' tastes for wine faded, except for those of European ancestry, and the post-Prohibition wine market remained feeble.

World War II proved kinder to the wine industry than had World War I. As grain products were severely rationed and allocated for food production, the supply of wine exceeded that of beer and spirits, and there was little competition from imports. Americans once again began drinking wine.

When the war ended, the energy and dynamism of a victorious country, the strongest and most affluent in the world, was unleashed. An entrepreneurial zeal revitalized the wine industry and led a new generation of would-be vintners to seek their fortunes amidst the vine-carpeted hills of northern California. Among them were Mario and John Trinchero.

RISING FROM ASHES

An old axiom in Napa Valley goes, "To make a small fortune in the wine industry, start with a large fortune."

While Mary and the kids shivered at the El Bonita Motel in 1948 and Mario kept the Sutter Home winery doors open late into the night in hopes of boosting sales, most other wineries in Napa Valley closed their doors for the evening, with their owners tucked warmly into plush, comfortable estate homes.

Pedigreed wineries like Inglenook and Beaulieu exemplified the wealthy, high-society vintners of the 1940s and 1950s. Even the winery owners a notch down from the aristocrats lived comfortable lives. Cesare Mondavi made a good enough living in his family's Charles Krug Winery to send his two sons, Robert and Peter, to Stanford in the 1930s.

Founded in 1900, Beaulieu Vineyard continued production right through Prohibition. By the late 1930s, Georges de Latour, Beaulieu's owner, had plenty of money to hire the now-famous André Tschelistcheff, a Russian émigré whose understanding of fine wine making and the nuances of Napa Valley *terroir* earned him a reputation as the dean of American winemakers. For 35 years, his work at Beaulieu set standards by which other wineries would be judged, both in product quality and technical advances. Georges died in 1940, but his widow, Madame de Latour, and her daughter, Helene de Pins, continued to enjoy their aristocratic lifestyles while their winemaker's wines earned medals and helped establish the Napa Valley as a source of premium wines.

Across the road from Beaulieu, the Inglenook Vineyard also traced its heritage back to Victorian days, and it had the stone structure and established acreage to prove it. A Finnish sea captain who made his fortune in the Alaskan fur trade, Gustav Niebaum, founded the winery in the 1880s, outfitting it with state-of-the-art fixtures and equipment. His Inglenook vineyard produced such impeccable wines that, in 1889, the Paris Exposition bestowed on it a special award for "excellence and purity." (Today, filmmaker Francis Ford Coppola owns the winery, under the name of Niebaum-Coppola Estates.)

Decades later, while the Trincheros whacked down weeds in front of their ramshackle barn, Niebaum's grandnephew, John Daniel, continued his family's prestigious legacy. From within the impressive stone walls of the Inglenook estate, Daniel refused to bottle inexpensive generic wines, a practice popular among other Napa wineries such as Beaulieu, Martini, and Charles Krug, which used them to help foot the bill for more costly premium wines. Daniel declined to follow suit and instead labeled Inglenook wines by variety and origin, producing and bottling them on the same estate where the grapes were grown—making Inglenook wines among the first true estate wines in California.

As a foreshadowing of what would later be commonplace in the state's wine industry, Daniel surprised the valley by selling his family's esteemed winery in 1964 to Louis Petri and United Vintners, a much larger concern. Despite a promise to maintain the Inglenook commitment to estate wines, the new owners had, within a year, produced generic wines under the Inglenook label, using grapes from the Central Valley, not Napa. Ultimately, Heublein, makers of Smirnoff vodka, acquired 80 percent of United Vintners. Inglenook's reputation disintegrated, and the family itself dissolved in its dust. John Daniel, whose heritage and vision of excellence had been so much a part of Napa aristocracy, died in 1970.

That same year, Bob Trinchero still made less than $100 a week at his family winery, just two miles down the road from the original Niebaum estate, and he was giddy with what was to be his first real success as a winemaker: Sutter Home's 1968 Amador County Zinfandel.

4

Ma 'n' Pa Set Up Shop

In 1948, Sutter Home Winery looked like it had during the final harvest 30 years earlier. On the second floor of the original winery building were old fermentation tanks, on the ground floor, a grape press and assorted storage tanks.

Nineteenth century wineries, without sophisticated, mechanized pumps, had been designed to take advantage of gravity flow. Grapes were crushed and fermented on an upper level and flowed down to storage tanks on a lower level. Although the Trincheros discarded many of the old, unusable tanks, they salvaged enough of them to accommodate their initial meager production.

In 1948, there were only a handful of wineries in Napa County (compared to about 300 today). Grapes competed with prunes, walnuts, tomatoes, and cattle for available acreage. And the varieties prevalent then, such as Carignane and Palomino, eventually gave way to "noble" varieties such as Chardonnay and Cabernet Sauvignon. In fact, during the 1940s and 1950s, wine grapes were generally classified as either "black" or "white," and neither fetched much money.

The late 1940s was a tough time for grape growers. Prices dropped from a 1946 high of $125 per ton to less than $50 per ton in 1947. Most California wine was sold in bulk by larger producers to smaller wineries or bottlers elsewhere in the United States. Jug wines constituted the largest sales category and sold for less than $1 per gallon.

BOTTLES UNCORKED

At Sutter Home, the Trincheros purchased all their dessert wines and some of their dry table wines in bulk. They produced a few varietal wines and a better class of jug wine at the winery. While Gallo operated its own glass plant, custom-producing its own bottles to eliminate markups and middlemen expenses, the Trinchero family applied their own cost-cutting bottling measures out of fiscal necessity: They obtained used bottles from a variety of larger vintners, washed and sterilized them, and then refilled them.

The practice of recycling bottles at Sutter Home started with their first vintage, when Mario, Bob, and, later, Roger drove from winery to winery collecting them wherever they could, a strategy that continued well into the 1970s. At times, it meant not just washing the bottles, but removing corks from them as well. As Darrell Corti, a friend and colleague of the Trincheros, recalls, "In 1972, Dick Peterson had just taken over at Beaulieu from André Tchelistcheff. He decided to make a Gamay Beaujolais— everyone started to make nouveau-type wines then. But they faced a challenge: How are we going to stop malolactic fermentation in the bottle? You can stop malolactic fermentation by adding chemicals, and one of them was fumaric acid. So they did. And it didn't taste good.

"What did they do? They dumped the wine. In those

days, since it was possible to actually recycle glass, and Sutter Home was the only place to recycle glass other than a
place in Berkeley, what they did at Beaulieu was to simply
take the foils off the bottles, put an extension on the
corker, drive the cork in, dump out the wine, and put the
bottles back in the cases. They gave the cases to Sutter
Home. Bob took the cases and asked me, 'How am I supposed to get the corks out?' I said, "You get a hook like
this,' " Corti says, curving his finger into a hooked position. "You convert that hook so it sticks up out of the
floor, put the bottle on top of the hook. Then Evalyn,
Bob's wife, pulled the bottle up, with the hook grabbing
and pulling out the cork. The hook was made so the cork
would stick on it, and the bottle pulled free. So, they
removed the corks, washed all the bottles, and recycled
them for Sutter Home wines."

RED OR WHITE

By the early 1950s, Sutter Home produced 52 different
wines, although locals joked that the winery had only two
tanks—one for white wine and one for red. Bob Trinchero
admits that wasn't far from the truth.

"We were the quintessential mom-and-pop winery,"
Bob recalls. "Sixty-five percent of our wine was sold out
the front door of our winery. If you could carry or roll a
container through our door, we'd fill it up for you. Customers would come in and ask for a particular wine, and
while my dad talked to them, I'd go in the back room and
slap on the right label." Thus, there often wasn't much difference between the Chablis and Sauternes, the Burgundy
and the Claret.

While John Trinchero made the wine and Mario sold

it, other family members did whatever was necessary to keep the family business afloat. Mary Trinchero worked 10-hour days on the bottling line, kept the books, and cooked meals in the kitchen behind the tasting room. Vera and Roger also helped out on the bottling line after school and on weekends, while older brother Bob performed more strenuous tasks like shoveling pomace or cleaning out tanks and barrels. After dinner, Mario, John, and their friends played cards—an Italian game called *pedro*—in the tasting room until late at night, in the event someone dropped by to buy a bottle of wine. (The Trincheros were the first vintners in the valley to offer free tastes and sales of their wines on the premises.)

GROWING UP IN NAPA VALLEY

"It snowed in the valley on Christmas Day," reminisces Vera. "This was our first year here, just three weeks after we arrived. The snow lasted pretty much all day. My mother said, all the years that she lived in New York, it never snowed on Christmas Day. It snowed before, or after, or for months during the winter. 'I had to come out to California' she said, 'to have snow on Christmas Day.' We spent the day over at Uncle John and Aunt Nina's house, away from the El Bonita cabin. It was comforting in a way, when I saw the snow that morning, because we were so used to it in New York."

Little did Vera know what had been so commonplace in New York was a rarity in their new home: It had been 11 years since snow last fell in the valley. "I played with the Huntsinger kids who lived next door. We made snowballs and had a blast," she adds. One of those kids, Jim Huntsinger, later grew up to work for various valley wineries, ending up today as Trinchero Family Estate's (TFE) senior vice president of production.

Mary never forgot that day when it snowed. "It was nearly 30 years later, at the Christmas party of '87," recalls her grandson Bobby Torres, one of Vera's boys, now a TFE vice president himself. "We had just hired Jim Huntsinger. My uncle Bob introduces him, saying 'Mom I want you to meet Jim Huntsinger, our new VP of production.' Grandma looks at Jim and slowly says, 'December twenty-fifth, nineteen forty-eight. You threw a snowball at our screen door." Jim turned pale, but quickly recovered. 'No, Mrs. Trinchero. Honest. That wasn't me. That was my brother!' he sputtered."

Not All Bad

Though Mary Trinchero cried throughout that first winter and into spring, the kids, being kids, were more resilient. In time, all of the Trincheros would find some redeeming qualities in the strange new land of Napa Valley.

"You know," says Vera with a sparkle in her voice, "it was an adventure for me. I missed my friends but it was amazing to walk out the door and see green! And see hawks, and see grass, and see trees. Before, we had to walk a block to Central Park to see green. Here, you open up the door and there it is. And I made friends with this gal, Jeanette White, who lived there at the El Bonita, too. She and I played long and hard. By the end of the summer I could walk barefoot on glass, my feet had become so tough. We went barefoot all summer long, and in back of the El Bonita Motel, we'd clamber over rocks and catch various blue-bellied lizards. I had a ball.

"One time, I remember going with Jeannette to the Assembly of God Church, her church. And we went to the service. Of course, my family was Catholic. Well, during the service, I kept looking around nervously. I thought I was going to go straight to hell. In those days you weren't supposed to know about anyone else's religion, let alone set foot in somebody else's church. I thought for sure God was going to strike me down for having a mortal sin on my soul. Boy, that was a scary morning! I kept telling Jeanette, I have to leave!"

Although he was just a toddler at the time, Roger also has fond memories of those early days. "I can smell the cellar and remember the feeling I had playing in the winery while my father worked. We had a dirt floor, and there was wine on the floor from spillage, and the smell permeated the whole cellar. I can remember that from a very early age. And I remember the eucalyptus trees, playing in the felled trees and enjoying myself immensely."

Little Hands Help Out

Mario Trinchero wasted no time introducing Mary, Vera, and Bob to the vintner's life. John and he crushed three tons of grapes during the 1948 harvest, Sutter Home's first in over 30 years, and there was other work to be done.

"My dad put me to work right away," Bob recalls. "I helped him bottle. It was just a few days after we came from New York. By that time, I thought it was something of an adventure, like a vacation. But as the months rolled by, I realized it wasn't."

Vera worked on the bottling line, too. "We'd come home from school and bottle on weekends. Bob was the official bottle handler, but Dad showed me how to apply the screw caps. First, I'd put the wet seals on. Do you know about the wet seals? The seals soaked in a big bucket. I'd slip the seals on top of the screw cap, and as they dried they'd shrink. I put the caps on the half-gallon and the gallon jugs and put them in the cases. Mary and Aunt Nina did the labeling. That was all hand done. And I'd put the jugs aside in the cases. Dad then stacked them at the front door, so when he loaded them up, the last to be loaded would be the first to deliver."

Vera also took care of her little brother, Roger. "He was only two and a half when we came here. I used to put him in a cardboard box and roll him back and forth on the conveyor belt to keep him amused," she remembers.

"Uncle John was the winemaker, and Dad was the salesman. We'd probably bottle once a week, when the orders came up. I remember one time we had a record bottling of 300 cases. That's quite a bit when everything was done manually. I got 25 cents an hour. I'd work about an hour a day, and then on Saturdays. We did most of the bottling on weekends, getting the orders ready for delivery on Monday."

When times got busy, which was rare, Mario occasionally hired someone to help out, though not always with much success. Vera rolls her eyes at the thought of one of the workers. "We had a glue machine that we passed the labels through. This guy, instead of passing it under the roller, like you're supposed to do to pick up the glue, he tried to skim it over the top."

From the first day, the whole family pitched in to make Mario's dream a reality. Even Mary, despite her reticence about moving to California, never stopped being a team player. "Dad and Mom worked really, really hard," Vera recalls. "They'd be up at 5:00 A.M. in the summer months, 6:00 A.M. in the winter months, and they'd work until 11 at night. But one thing they always did, which is so Italian, was power-nap in the afternoon, after lunch. It would reenergize them. And they did this regularly until the day each died. They'd nap and then they'd wake up and," Vera snaps her fingers, "like that, they were ready to go again."

Tensions Arise

Even in the closest of families, spats erupt from time to time, and the Trincheros were no different. In a famous winery legend, the Mondavi brothers, Robert and Peter, came to blows, literally, at their family's Charles Krug Winery, and as a result, Robert Mondavi left the family business and created his own winery, now hugely successful. Mario Trinchero's battle with his brother John was far less dramatic, but Vera recalls how the tensions created by her uncle John colored her, her brothers', and her mother's world.

"The only one none of us could get along with was Uncle John. He was a bear. He was not a happy man. He had two daughters; one lived back East. He didn't have a son, no one to leave the business to. He was just a grouchy old man. Dad was the only person who got along with him, really. I remember the one and only time I saw my father ready to come to blows with Uncle John. Roger was six years old, and Uncle John was tired of Roger following him around, so he took Roger and threw him in an empty wine tank and shut the door. It was terrible. The poor little guy was pretty scared. My dad was furious. 'Okay, stand up!' he said to Uncle John. 'Don't you ever touch my children again!' Dad was ready to kill him. Dad was short but he was very muscular, very athletic. Uncle John knew my dad could beat the hell out of him if he wanted to. So he backed off. But Roger wasn't the only one he picked on. He treated my brother Bob really badly. Me, he didn't even pay attention to. You know, I was a girl, a nothing. And he and my mother used to get into fights, too. So we were all kind of glad when he later sold his shares to Dad and Mom in 1960 and retired."

Despite Uncle John's disposition, he was the real wine-maker. "My dad was all business and he really didn't do that much as far as making the wine," notes Vera. As time went on, "Bob learned more and more from Uncle John, and soon Bob became the winemaker. Bob took a few courses at UC Davis, but basically his knowledge was all hands-on."

John Moves Out, Bob Moves Up

In 1954, Bob Trinchero graduated from high school. The following year, he joined the Air Force and in 1956, married his high school sweetheart, Evalyn Jones. After returning from Air Force duty in 1958, he asked his father for a job.

"I was fresh out of the service, and I had a family to support, but my father said, 'You know, Bob, there really isn't much of a future in the wine business. The winery really can't afford you, but we'll give you a part-time job until you can find something more meaningful, something with a future.' "

It's no wonder Mario considered the wine industry a business with no future. In 1960, there were only 15 wineries in Napa Valley. Of those, most bottled only a few hundred cases of wine annually, while the Big Five—Beringer, Beaulieu, Inglenook, Christian Brothers, and Charles Krug—dominated the market. It was a sobering contrast to 1890, when more than 140 wineries operated in Napa Valley and the Leuenbergers painted the words Sutter Home Winery on the roof of John Thomann's initial enterprise.

In 1960, while the smaller wineries limped along and the handful of larger wineries boomed, John Trinchero decided to retire. Mario and Bob bought his share in the winery, and although he had no formal wine-making training, Bob became the winemaker, while his wife, Eva-lyn, worked full-time alongside Mary Trinchero on the bottling line.

ROGER AND VERA GROW UP

During this period, two important characters were missing from the daily events at the winery: Roger and Vera. Their experiences outside the winery would help shape them and their interactions within the winery today.

Roger Leaves Home

In the early 1960s, Roger was a star linebacker on the foot-ball team at St. Helena High School, which earned him a four-year scholarship to UCLA. His parents, knowing he would be the first Trinchero to attend college, had scraped and saved $3,000 over the years for his tuition. Since the scholarship would effectively pay for Roger's education, Mario and Mary instead used the money to give him a spe-cial going-away present: a red Corvette, the only thing in the world he ever asked for. "What were they thinking?" brother Bob exclaims, "Sending an 18-year-old football player to Los Angeles in a red Corvette?" Roger played two years at UCLA and then transferred to a state univer-sity in Utah on another scholarship. But his football days never went beyond college. "I was too small to go pro," he says, "and after 15 years of playing football, I was burned out. I was later offered $150 a week," he adds, "to play for a semipro team in the San Francisco Bay Area. A whole $150 a week."

After college, Roger was drafted into the army. Other than his army days, an occasional construction job, and a one-month stint selling vacuum cleaners door-to-door, Roger's only real work experience has been the winery.

"In the army, I learned how to skate," says Roger, "to get by. The army didn't teach me anything, really. It was an opportunity to be exposed to a wider variety of people than I had seen in college. And it gave me a broader knowledge of the world—I saw Georgia and Vietnam," he remarks with a slight grin. Unlike many draftees, Roger served after he graduated from college, at the relatively mature age of 22. In 1972, after discharge from the army, Roger joined the winery full-time.

Vera Becomes a Working Mother

Vera never worked much in the winery, except as a kid. As an adult, necessity forced her to go outside the family to find work.

"I didn't have that much to do with the winery then. The winery couldn't afford to hire me. Bob and Evalyn just barely made it with Mom and Dad. In 1955, I worked part-time for Judge Palmer, a justice of the peace who was an attorney in town." After graduating from high school the next year, Vera worked for the judge full-time. "I worked a total of 24 years as a legal secretary. In 1970, when Judge Palmer died, another law firm in Napa Valley took over, and I worked for them until 1979. On Fridays, though, I still worked at the winery, doing the correspondence. Finally, in 1979, brother Bob said, 'Vera, I think we can afford to pay you if you would come and work full-time.' And so I did."

While Roger shipped off to Georgia and Southeast Asia, Vera raised two young sons, Tony and Bobby Torres.

Their father had been a schoolmate of Bob's and labored in construction when Vera married him.

"I was 20 when I got married," Vera says. "I had Tony in May of '59, and Bobby in 1960. They were 10 months, three weeks apart. Tony was still in diapers when I had Bobby." Today, Tony is TFE's vice president of administration and Bobby is vice president of operations.

"My dad was one of the first friends of my Uncle Bob," recalls Bobby. "When Uncle Bob moved here, he was a street-tough, New York kid who dressed funny. My dad was one of his first friends. So my mother knew my dad for a long time because my Uncle Bob would ride his bike over to his house; they'd hang out, go over to the river, shoot slingshots. As they got older, Bob would steal a little wine from the winery and they'd drink that in high school. My dad was a quarterback; my Uncle Bob was his wide receiver. They were in the same class in high school. And, of course, they later became brothers-in-law."

Vera's marriage didn't last. "We were both in college when our parents divorced," says Tony. "When they told us, we said good. You guys are great people when separate. Together you're like oil and water." Around this same time, Vera joined her family full-time at the winery. She became a valuable asset at a time when the Trincheros were about to feel the full impact of White Zinfandel's success.

Tony and Bobby Pitch In

Even before Vera joined the winery full-time, her own kids helped out in the family business. Tony and Bobby Torres first recall putting the plastic seals on the caps in 1967, when they were around eight years old, just as their mother and uncles before them had done. Later on, the brothers became useful in other ways.

"One of the jobs they gave me was to go inside one of these oak ovals, these tanks. Each one has a little gate on it. Uncle Bob couldn't fit through the gate, but I was a 15-year-old kid and just the right size," recalls Bobby. "He and Steve Bertolucci, the first winemaker that we hired, handed me a scraper. 'Get in there and scrape all the tartrates off the inside.' So in I went." Bobby shakes his head with a reminiscing grin. Tartrates are potassium bitartrate crystals that form on a cask, cork, or in a bottle, and naturally occur in wine. Over time, they build up and need to be removed.

"As kids, we all had to do that," added Tony, referring to himself and the other sons and daughters of his generation. "There was no OSHA!" says Bobby, whose job as vice president of operations includes overseeing worker safety. "Today, you'd have to have a permit, another guy with a rope around your waist, and safety harnesses. You couldn't do that now. Especially with kids."

Bobby continues, "So here I am. Thank God I wasn't claustrophobic. You get in this thing. You can barely stand up. It's got an oval bottom so your footing is lousy. And you're moving your arms, scraping all the while. This is the wine business," Bobby laughs, "the romantic wine business!

"Being a kid, you always get the duties that no one wants to do, whether it's washing floors with chlorine, scraping the tanks out, or sulphuring the barrels, which I really didn't like doing. Because of expansion and contraction, the wine may spill out at the bung and leak down the side. Mold may start to grow and attract fruit flies. So you need to clean off the barrels to remove the mold and keep the fruit flies from coming.

"We didn't have a lot of barrels back then, because we didn't have a lot of space. There was a small area by the cellar where the barrels were stacked up. It was very dark. So

Steve stirs up this mixture, which is sulfur dioxide and water, or metabisulfide, hands me a rag, and says 'Okay, Bobino,' which is what he called me then, 'you get to wipe the barrels off.' " Bobby moves his hands around, like Pat Morita in *The Karate Kid:* Wax on, wax off. Only in this case, it's wipe off, wipe off.

"So there's no light in there, where the barrels are. It's basically black." Bobby wipes off the barrels with his imaginary rag as he speaks. "You stick your hand in there," he says as he extends his arm, "and it's nothing but black widow webs. You go in farther and you can just feel them. They're not like regular webs. They're really tough—with a kind of ropy feeling. I don't know how many times I pulled out my hand to see a big one crawling up my arm. Forget about having a glove on. It's creepy, but you do it."

As Bobby said: This was the wine business, the glamorous wine business.

BOB, THE WINEMAKER

While Vera raised kids and Roger fought a war, Bob was totally immersed in running the family winery. Bob had already spent four years in the Air Force, at Winslow, Arizona, having signed up in 1955. Like Roger, his appreciation of service life is limited. "I learned how to make a bed," he jokes, "and that I wasn't going to reenlist. That's it." At the end of his first year, he married his high school sweetheart, and they shared a small apartment off base. "Being in the Air Force was just a job. I'd drive to work at the base every day and drive home at night."

Despite the rigorous life of the armed services, the meager military pay each of the brothers earned was more than they had ever made. Bob's monthly check of $97 amply covered the $35 a month rent on the apartment, while his wife Evalyn brought in a heftier monthly salary of $146 at a job in town. Life was good. Years later, the army would pay Roger a monthly check of $380, which included combat pay. At the time, the brothers considered these amounts a fortune.

Bob's resume is as slim as Roger's and Vera's. The only real work experience outside the winery he's ever known is his four-year run in the Air Force and summers at the prune hydrator. Oddly enough, this lack of exposure encouraged the Trincheros to figure things out for themselves, on their own terms, and to come up with solutions in their own way. Bob's beginnings as a winemaker illustrate this.

"At the beginning, I really didn't know what I was doing," Bob recalls, "I wasn't a very good winemaker. When I came home from the service in 1958, I started working for the winery because it was the only opportunity I had. In 1960, Uncle John wanted to retire. Remember that my dad and Uncle John were not young men when they came out here. In 1960, my dad was already 61 years old, and my uncle was 68 years old. My dad said to me, can you make wine? Well, I'd followed my Uncle John around enough, so I said, 'Oh, yeah, I think I can do it.'

"Well, I really couldn't. Louis Martini helped me out," continues Bob. Louis Martini's St. Helena winery, built in 1933, sits directly across the street from Sutter Home. An old-school Italian, Martini was recognized as one of Napa Valley's most skilled winemakers and, like the Trincheros, never flashy or pretentious. "We'd see each other at certain meetings. Or my pump would break down, and I'd go across the street and borrow a part from him. He was always very nice to me. He was really the number one winemaker back then, very highly prized and respected. For someone like that to take 15 or 20 minutes of his time to discuss wine or explain things to me, I thought that was a big deal. And it helped me a lot. Joe Heitz helped also, and several other winemakers. But especially Louis Martini. He was very nice. Later, I became friends with his winemaker Bill Fuller. Louis was, of course, the winemaker, but Bill did all the work. Bill was a chemist, and he allowed me to go over there and watch him do stuff in the lab."

Winemakers have always learned their trade from each other by sharing information. "There was no feeling of rivalry—my God, no," says Bob. "First of all, at that time Louis Martini sold 300,000 cases and I'm at six. I was simply no competition. There was never a feeling of rivalry. There is today, but only among the larger wineries. Beringer and Robert Mondavi are here in the valley, and we do compete with them on the market, but we're all friends. We all talk to each other, and we all compete in the same marketplace, but we understand that."

Bob, as he says, was a sponge back then, absorbing as much information as he could, from wherever he could. Once Uncle John dropped out, Bob's thirst for knowledge intensified.

"When we took over in March, and my dad and I bought my uncle's share of the winery, I signed up for a two-week short course at Davis. Of course, the classes were very small. Today, they have an auditorium, but then it was maybe 15 of us. I learned a lot. I went to lunches and talked to people. I had dinner with Maynard Amerine, one of the leading wine scholars, and he gave me a lot of hints. I went to the library. I read and read and read. I had one book that was my bible, it was by Cruess, called *Wine*. I would read every chapter. Then my uncle left me his formulas for vermouth. Vermouth was very big for us. So I just developed into it."

CHANGING TIDES

As Bob learned his craft in the early 1960s, the winery struggled. Mario was turned down for a $5,000 bank loan. He briefly entertained a $100,000 offer to sell the winery, but when the prospective buyer tried to shave $10,000 from his original price, Mario broke off negotiations. For the Trinchero family, things once again looked pretty gloomy.

However, during this era, American lifestyles changed rapidly. With a lilting *"Bon appétit!"* Julia Child arrived on the airwaves as *The French Chef.* Jackie Kennedy installed a French chef in the White House. Jet airplanes, introduced in the 1950s, were now loaded with Americans traveling abroad—the most ever to do so. Paris and Rome were among the foremost destinations. And, while Americans experienced fine dining and premium wines in the White House and overseas, foreign visitors in record numbers brought their cultural habits to the United States, favoring the nation's sophisticated centers of New York, San Francisco, and Los Angeles, among other large cities (Caplow et al. 2000).

All of this helped produce a greater exposure to, and appreciation of, fine wines and fine dining. Wine lost its reputation as cheap swill and started to be perceived as the cultured drink Europeans had always considered it to be. During the 1960s, Americans also enjoyed more leisure time. The majority of jobs shifted from blue collar to white collar. For both labor groups, the customary half day of work on Saturdays disappeared by 1960. White-collar workers not only rose in numbers, they also arrived at their desks later and worked shorter hours. Vacation days increased, as did the number of paid holidays and sick leave days. For the homemaker, supermarkets and automation in the form of vacuum cleaners, microwave ovens, and dishwashers greatly simplified household tasks, allowing for both more leisure time at home and an increase in women in the workplace. The entire population became more educated, and 1960 marked the beginning of a spike in both high school diplomas and higher-education degrees.

Perhaps Mario sensed that with these substantial changes in lifestyle, wine drinking would increase, which encouraged him to stick to his guns. Or perhaps bankers began to see the light, becoming themselves a winemaker's target market.

In 1963, Mario finally obtained a $32,000 loan from Wells Fargo Bank, enabling Sutter Home to retire its debts, make needed improvements to the winery, and purchase higher-quality grapes. Sutter Home had survived a shaky period and, in keeping with this country's own growth, was on the brink of some momentous changes.

But even with a new loan, Mario was ever frugal. "It was a different mentality," Roger adds, "like Mom and her envelopes. She always kept these envelopes to pay the bills. One for electricity, one for rent, one for water, and so forth. She would tuck away enough money each month to pay the bills."

Bob nods in agreement. "In 1966, Evalyn and I lived on the second floor of my parents' house. We had just adopted a second kid, so now we had two infants. I found a house I wanted to buy for $11,500. But I didn't have a penny. A bank loaned me $7,500, but I was still $4,000 short, with closing fees and such. So I told the Realtor, you go out and find me a loan. A new savings and loan just opened up in Napa, and the Realtor managed to get me a loan from them for $2,000. But that still wasn't enough. I told my mother I needed another $2,000, and had no idea where I would get it. Quietly, she went to her room. She came back with an envelope that contained exactly $2,000. That was all the money she had saved in 18 years, from 1948 to 1966, and she gave it to me."

PART TWO

EUREKA! LIQUID GOLD AND THE BLUSH RUSH

5

Zinfandel and the Corti Connection

Darrell Corti may not be a household name, but among California vintners and the cognoscenti of food and wine, he is a prominent character. In 1999, *Saveur* magazine added him and his family's Corti Brothers market (a "gastronomic emporium" in Sacramento) to their "*Saveur* 100," a listing of their favorite food, people, places and things—and called Corti "The Man Who Knows Everything About Food and Wine."

Corti speaks seven languages. In addition to being a paid consultant to the Italian Trade Commission, he is an international wine judge. For decades, this walking encyclopedia has generously offered himself as an unofficial, occasional consultant to many vintners and food purveyors throughout northern California and the world. He has also been described as opinionated, professorial, and pontifical, but extremely knowledgeable, a man with both a good palate and a good heart. Ever controversial, Corti can be quietly reserved, enthusiastically supportive, or pointedly direct, and he's famous for helping develop the Sierra foothills wine industry. In one speech, he called the area "Amateur County," which was his way of saying to local vintners, "You need to improve." When the books on California wine history are written about this era, Darrell Corti will be part of them.

Erudite and never bashful, Corti's credo is to further culinary education. When it comes to wine, his catholic perspective might surprise some, but it's an attitude shared by the Trincheros and the foundation of California's post-Prohibition wine industry. "Leon Adams said some 25 years ago," Corti advises, "that there's got to be two kinds of wine: everyday wine and Sunday wine. And wine should cost not more than a gallon of milk." Leon Adams, cofounder of the Wine Institute at the time Prohibition was repealed, was instrumental in drafting many of the laws pertaining to wine today.

On hearing this, Bob asks Corti, "How much is a gallon of milk?" About $3, Corti tells him. "That sounds about right," Bob agrees. "We can produce good wine for $1.99 a bottle. The consumer shouldn't have to pay much more than that for a decent bottle of wine. Today, a wine's value is all about image."

KINDRED SPIRITS

Clearly, Bob and Corti are two men bonded by the same perspective: Wine can and should be an affordable everyday beverage of good quality. When "The Man Who Knows Everything About Food and Wine" first walked into the Trinchero tasting room in 1963, he initiated a chain reaction of fortuitous events that would forever impact the Trinchero family business.

As Corti recollects, "In 1962, Joe Heitz, who became a prominent winemaker in Napa Valley, delivered wine to me. In those days, winemakers weren't like they are now.

Winemakers would buy the grapes, make the wine, bottle the wine, sell the wine, and deliver the wine. Joe had a regular delivery run up to Sacramento, where he sold wines to us at Corti Brothers and then he continued on to Davis and Woodland. One day I asked him, 'Joe, where can I get someone in Napa Valley to bottle us some decent jug wine?' Joe himself wasn't set up for bottling jug wines, but he suggested a nearby winery, Sutter Home, which did sell jug wines.

"One Sunday, my father Frank, my Uncle Gino, and I paid a visit to Sutter Home. Nowadays, there's a big and a little part of their tasting room. Back then the big part was a section of the winery itself, and the little part was the actual tasting room. Behind the winery area was a room that functioned as the kitchen, office, and laboratory. So we sat down there with Bob and Mario, and we tasted some wine. It was good."

In 1965, Sutter Home began to produce gallon and half gallon jug wines for the Corti family's "Tosca" house brand, and Bob and Corti became friends, united by their love of wine.

A WINEMAKER COMES OF AGE

"After Darrell came into my life," says Bob, "we always talked. At this point, I was more of a sponge than anything else. Darrell has this total recall memory, a photographic mind, and I got a lot of information from him. So one thing led to another."

During the mid-1960s, as Bob Trinchero gained confidence as a winemaker, he upgraded the quality of Sutter Home's wines, eliminating some of the generic jug bottlings and replacing them with varietals. The varietals garnered increasing praise, while the jug wines paid the bills. Bob was pleased. Finally, his wines attracted attention.

"I was really into making wine then. I would say that from the time I took over in 1960, which was when I made my first vintage, to the time I made the first Amador Zinfandel in 1968, eight vintages, I became a winemaker," says Bob, almost in amazement. "I really started to put all the pieces together, because, from then on, all the wines were really first class.

"Darrell had a lot to do with that. I'll tell you this one thing he did for me. He bought me wine, other peoples' wine. You have to remember, I'm making fifty bucks a week, and I had a wife to support. So I couldn't afford to buy other wine. When Darrell tasted my wine, he was very diplomatic. He didn't say my wine tasted like horse piss. But he did say, 'Bob, I brought you a couple bottles of wine and I want you to taste them,' without coming out and saying directly, 'Bob, this is what Zinfandel is supposed to taste like.' So I tasted them and said, 'Wow, this tastes a lot different.'

"What I didn't realize was, our winery was badly infected with bacteria. Remember, the casks we used were the same casks that were in the winery since before Prohibition. The owners just closed it up in 1918 and left everything there until 1948. Well, naturally there was all this bacterial spoilage. As a 12-year-old kid, I used to collect reeds from the river, dry them out, and fill them in between the staves, 'cause I was the only one small enough to fit through the little doors. Then my uncle would put the steam in there and stretch it. Those tanks smelled terrible! I still remember the smell in my nose. Well, you put wine in there. What do you expect the wine to smell like? So there was some bacterial thing going on, but you get used to it. And you drink your wine, and you think it's okay. Until you drink other wines. That was the first thing Darrell did. He exposed me to other wines.

"Louis Martini had a bacterial thing, but his was a good thing," notes Bob, referring to his old friend, one of the "who's who" of Napa Valley vintners. "It's called a winery character, and you can almost identify wineries by their winery character. Nobody changed barrels back then. You used the same tanks over and over. And over the years, you develop a winery character. Louis Martini had a good one. I had a bad one.

"Anyway, Darrell would bring me six or seven bottles of wine. We'd taste them together, and I'd say, 'Wow, this stuff is really pretty good.' And then what happened, of course, is that I would realize the flaws of my own wine. See, if you keep drinking your own wine, you become accustomed to these flaws. You're insular. It's not that they were bad wines, they were just off a little bit, and somebody who really understood wine would notice the flaws. But I didn't realize my wine was off. When Darrell and I tasted other wines, that really opened up my mind. Wow! So this is what Cabernet is supposed to taste like. Tasting these other wines helped a lot."

EARLY ESCAPADES

Bob's wine-tasting experiences soon paid off. He developed a good palate. Corti recalls one particularly great product that Bob discovered on his own and subsequently bottled for Corti Brothers. "In those days, everybody bought wine in bulk from every other winery. Winemakers exchanged wines they made with wines from other winemakers, so they could all have complete lines of wine," explains Corti. "Besides his own wines, Bob also delivered or bottled wines he didn't make. Winemakers like John and Mario Gemello bought vermouth and Marsala from Sutter Home, and Bob bought what he needed, as he needed it, to supplement his line of Sutter Home wines."

A Shrewd Buy

"In 1969, our store sold wine that Bob bought from Gemello's winery in Mountain View. Bob brought the wine back to Sutter Home in barrels stenciled with the words 'LEMON EXTRACT.' They were perfectly good containers." As with scavenging and recycling wine bottles, the Trincheros used any containers they could, even if they weren't meant for wine.

Back then, Corti drove from his store in Sacramento to Napa Valley once a month. "I went to Gemello's and bought some old Cabernets," Bob told Corti on one visit.

"In those days, old Cabs didn't sell very well," Corti adds. "But Bob said he tasted them and he liked them, so he bought 100 gallons, which he put into two 50 gallon barrels." Corti reaches out as if grabbing a glass, "Let me taste it. Holy s—!" Corti is a man not easily impressed, but when he is, he eagerly expresses himself. "This was really good wine. 'Bob,' I said to him, 'that's *really* good!' "

Bob was clearly developing the palate of a good winemaker. The wine he bought from Gemello was a blend of 1959 and 1960 Cabernet from Saratoga. But, as Bob told Corti, the wine was quite costly. He wanted $1.50 a gallon for it. Corti agreed that it was a very high price. "Bob asked me, 'What do you think we can sell a wine like this for?' I told him that if he bottled it, I would buy half. 'All right,' he said, 'that will relieve the pressure at home.' "

Then Bob asked Corti what he would sell the wine for. "I told him I'd sell it for $2.79 a bottle," recalls Corti.

"Remember, at that time, reserve wines were selling for less. So $2.79 was a bit pricey." As Bob and Corti finished their price discussion, Mario walked into the winery through the tasting room's swinging door. It was five o'clock, closing time. "Don't you want to stay for a drink?" asked Mario.

"A drink from Mario meant a martini," notes Corti. "He was a terrific martini maker."

Corti continues the story: "So Bob says, 'Hey, Dad, Darrell just bought half of this Cabernet that I bought from Gemello.' Mario replied casually, 'Wonderful. What are you going to sell it for?' So I told him we were both going to sell it for the same price, $2.79 a bottle.

"Mario took off like a Roman candle!" recalls Corti. " 'At $2.79 a bottle, I'll have that wine around for 40 years! I'm gonna go broke! You'll drive me into bankruptcy! You can't sell a wine for $2.79 a bottle. No one's gonna buy a wine at that price!' "

In fact, Gemello's Cabernet sold so well that Bob bought another 500 gallons of it. "This time," says Corti, "since Gemello now had a cask that was diminished by the previous 100 gallons taken out of it, he went down the road to San Martin Winery and bought some 1962 ruby Cabernet to top off the cask." Bob bought this 500-gallon blend, bottled it, and in the late 1970s sold the last 25 cases to a customer from Berkeley who bought them at $25 dollars a bottle.

"After that," adds Corti, "Mario Gemello got smart."

By that time, Bob bought fewer wines from Gemello. He instead focused on making his own good wines and, more often than not, succeeded.

Vermouth Resurrected

One day in 1973, Bob asked Corti, "What do you do with old red vermouth and old white vermouth?"

"New owners had just bought the Bartolucci winery, also in Napa Valley," explains Corti, "so the Bartoluccis had to move everything out of it. They came across two pallets of vermouth, dry white and sweet red. They bought the vermouth from Sutter Home, but never touched it." Sutter Home didn't have the greatest reputation for red and white wines in the early days, but it had a strong following for their fortified wines—sherry and vermouth—and also for vinegars.

"So the Bartoluccis call up Bob and say, 'Look, we have to get this stuff out of here, come down and get this vermouth.' Bob says, 'But you bought it. You bought it a long time ago.'

" 'Yeah, but we've never used it, and we don't know what to do with it, so come down and pick it up it. We'll just give it to you.' So they gave it back to Sutter Home.

"Bob calls me up one morning to tell me he now has all this vermouth. 'Do this,' I tell him, 'open the bottles, put it back to bulk, and I'll come take a look at it.' "

A few days later, Corti tastes the vermouth. "It was delicious. It was absolutely delicious." Bob didn't know what he was going to do with it, so Corti quickly jumps in. "I'll buy all of it," he says. "What are you going to sell it to me for?"

"Well, you know, it cost a lot of money. . . ." Bob replies to his good friend. "How about $12 a case?"

"Okay, sold," says Corti, and tells Bob to wash the original bottles and refill them. "They were wonderful-looking bottles—flint glass, punted bottles made by Owens of Illinois, with screw caps." Once the bottles were refilled, they ended up with 100 cases of vermouth.

The two men decide to give the vermouth the noble name of *Cantina Vecchia,* meaning "Old Cellar." Bob had labels printed up and started gluing them to the bottles when a hiccup in their plans occurred. "The Bureau of Alcohol, Tobacco and Firearms [BATF] told us we couldn't use the word *old* on a wine, because such an age reference is not provable," explains Corti. "Vintage-dated is okay, but you can't say *old*." (Faced with the same problem, Gallo changed the name of its Old Decanter Sherry to Sheffield.)

Bob doesn't know what to do, so Corti suggests: "Ask the BATF to give the labels to you as a use-up. You'll never use the word *old* again, but you'd like permission to sell what already is done." The BATF agreed.

Bob delivers the bottles of Cantina Vecchia to Corti Brothers, who sold them for $2.19 each. "I will never sell a wine that was that good again," Corti says. "It was terrific wine—bottle-aged vermouth." Once again, Bob found himself in the right place at the right time. And Corti was there with him.

1967 Vinegar

What did people in Napa Valley think of Sutter Home back then? "Not much," bluntly replies Corti. "Why? Because they made vinegar. Behind the office was the bottle-washing room and the vinegar room. There were people who came to Sutter Home to buy vermouth and vinegar— they made fantastic ones—but not to buy wines."

During his early years with the Trincheros, Corti says he got them into "all sorts of escapades," one of which involved Giurlani and Brothers, a San Francisco family that owned a company called Star Foods, makers of Star pickled peppers, vinegar, capers, and other Italian products. In 1940, their Star olive oil was the number three olive oil sold in the United States. Since 1995, the Borges Group, a

Spanish exporter of Mediterranean foods, has owned the Star brand.

"But this was in 1967 or '68," Corti recalls. "At that time, sherry wine vinegar was just coming into the United States. The first importer, a man named Frederick Bonsal Seggerman, imported a vinegar called Osborne from the sherry district," explains Corti, emphasizing the Spanish pronunciation (oss-boor-nay), "It was a great revelation. In those days, the sherry producers didn't want anyone to know they made vinegar. The Consejo Regulador [the controlling council of Spain's sherry industry] didn't want anyone to talk about vinegar. But they did make vinegar, and they sold it. Why was the idea of winemakers making vinegar shunned?" asks Corti rhetorically. "Vinegar was spoiled wine. That's what people think. But vinegar is *not* spoiled wine," he emphasizes. "Vinegar is wine that has gone to completion. As scholar Maynard Amerine was fond of saying, 'God gave us two things: grapes and vinegar. Wine is a halfway house.' "

Today, chefs and cooks clamor for specialty vinegars: aged balsamic vinegars from Modena; raspberry and other fruit vinegars; champagne vinegar from France; rice vinegars from Asia, and sherry vinegars. But back in 1967, such specialty vinegars were just being discovered.

"This sherry vinegar was very, very, very fast moving. It was pale amber in color. Everyone wanted sherry wine vinegar," describes Corti. "The Giurlanis wanted to get into the sherry vinegar business. They bought wine and sherry from Lustau, a firm that sold wine as a private label, as a buyers-own-brand label. So, in 1968, they said, 'Let's ask Lustau, our sherry producer, to send us some sherry vinegar.'

"The sherry vinegar arrives in black, Spanish glass

bottles, and inside, the vinegar itself is very dark in color, black in color. 'Oh, my God!' they said. 'Something must have happened.' Because the sherry vinegar they wanted was the light amber kind, the only one they had known. What they got was 250 cases of vinegar that's inkwell black. They knew I was going to Spain the following year, so they said to me, 'Look, why don't you do us a favor. Go see Lustau and go see the vinegar producer.' "

As it turns out, Lustau only *bottled* the vinegar; it didn't *make* the vinegar. "Sherry producers do make vinegar, though they don't make a lot of it. But there are specific sherry vinegar producers, and that's where this sherry vinegar came from. So we go to this bodega on the walls of the city of Tarifa. This old man opens what looks like a garage, and inside are all these barrels of vinegar. I say to him, 'You know, the Giurlanis are quite disappointed in the vinegar you sent. And he was astounded. 'Why?' he asked. 'I sent them my best vinegar! I gave them the vinegar before I actually refreshed the solera. It was very, very old vinegar.'

"So I said, 'Well, you know what they wanted was vinegar like the Osbornes are selling, the pale amber vinegar.'

" 'Why didn't they tell me that?' the man cried, almost in pain. 'That's normal vinegar—I gave them my *best* vinegar.' "

The Giurlanis sat on 250 cases of vinegar they considered inferior. "The vinegar looks like balsamic vinegar and it tastes like balsamic vinegar. No one knew what to do with it," says Corti. "They ask me who they can sell this vinegar to."

Corti leans back casually, "I said, there's a friend of mine down in Napa Valley, Bob Trinchero. He makes vinegar. *Maybe* he would take it off your hands for a dollar a case. They said okay. Of course, they had paid a lot of money for this stuff. A lot of money in those days was $6 a case."

Corti contacted Bob, who wasn't entirely convinced, but he thought he could try to use the vinegar and, even more important, the bottles. "So again, as with wine bottles, the Trincheros had to open all the bottles, pour everything back to bulk, and recycle the bottles. They washed the bottles to reuse them."

From his family's experience making good-quality vinegars, Bob knew that the dark, black sherry vinegar was superb, but it wasn't what people wanted. So Bob had an idea. He took the Sutter Home white wine vinegar and mixed it with the dark sherry vinegar, which diluted the color to the amber hue then in demand. As Corti, says, "People liked it. It was a very good solera." As a result, the Sutter Home Sherry Wine Vinegar became the only sherry wine vinegar ever bottled in California.

Which brings the topic back to the issue of the black Spanish bottles that originally held the sherry vinegar. Bob looked around and wondered what he would be able to do with all those bottles, which held 750 milliliters. "In those days," explains Corti, "the 750-milliliter bottle was an illegal size and could only be used in California but not shipped out of state." (Until the metric system was adopted by the United States, bottle sizes were in quarts only. Wines were sold as four-fifths of a quart. Anything other than four-fifths of a quart was fine to sell intrastate, but illegal for interstate sales. When the metric system was embraced, then everything went to 750 milliliters, and the four-fifths quart became illegal.)

"Since the bottles were not officially sized bottles, they could be sold only in California and not out of state. We used them for a wine that Bob made in 1969, after Bob first bought Zinfandel from Ken Deaver," Corti says, leading into his most important escapade with Bob Trinchero.

DEAVER'S GRAPES

Some of Bob's wines may have been a bit off, but a few made their mark among fine-wine drinkers. Bob gained speed as a winemaker.

In 1968, Bob complained to Corti about the escalating prices of Napa Valley grapes, which reached an unprecedented level of $200 a ton (compared to today's prices of over $2,000 per ton for topflight Chardonnay, Cabernet, and Merlot). Corti told Bob that high-quality, inexpensive Zinfandel grapes were available in Amador County, in the Sierra foothill gold country east of Sacramento, and offered Bob a bottle of 1965 Amador County Zinfandel made by a winemaker friend named Charlie Myers, an English professor at Sacramento City College (who was later to found Harbor Winery).

Bob hadn't the faintest idea where Amador County was, but the wine, made from 85-year-old vines grown in Amador's Shenandoah Valley, dazzled him. It was virtually black in color, with a huge bouquet of ripe, spicy, blackberry fruit, a thick, chewy texture, and incredibly intense, robust flavors. Bob thought it was one of the finest wines he had ever tasted.

A few weeks later, Corti and Myers took Bob to Amador to meet Ken Deaver, the grower whose fruit Myers used to make his 1965 Zinfandel. Deaver was a member of a pioneering Amador County family who first settled in the region in the 1850s, shortly after the discovery of gold at nearby Sutter's Mill. Deaver's family initially planted Mission grapes on their Shenandoah Valley property; then, in the 1880s, they began to cultivate Zinfandel.

Early Sierra Vines

Many of the fortune seekers who flocked to the Sierra foothills to prospect for gold were European immigrants, especially Italians and Serbians. They brought with them their love of red wine and, upon their arrival in the gold country, planted grapevines. After the mines ran dry, many remained in the area to make their livings as grape growers and winemakers.

By the 1890s, there were over 100 small wineries in Amador, El Dorado, Calaveras, Placer, and Nevada Counties (the area known as the Mother Lode). Most specialized in the hearty red wines for which the region's warm climate and poor, decomposed granite soils are ideally suited.

Unfortunately, Prohibition destroyed this vibrant frontier wine community and, unlike the north coast wine industry, it remained dormant even after the repeal of Prohibition. Only one winery, D'Agostini, survived, and vineyard land dwindled to a few hundred acres, its scant production purchased primarily by Italian-American home winemakers from Sacramento and San Francisco's North Beach district.

Thus, when Bob Trinchero arranged to purchase 20 tons of Zinfandel from Ken Deaver in 1968, Sutter Home became the first north coast winery to produce commercial wine from Sierra foothill grapes.

The Zen of Zin

Bob's enthusiasm was somewhat quixotic. Not only was Amador County unknown to wine sellers and consumers,

Zinfandel at the time had a rather lowly reputation. Although the wine enjoyed a period of prestige in the late nineteenth century as California's answer to French Bordeaux reds (it was often labeled "Claret") and won awards at international competitions, it was largely forgotten after Prohibition. A new generation of grape growers and winemakers, anxious to establish California's reputation, turned to classic French varieties like Cabernet Sauvignon, and relegated Zinfandel to a secondary role as a rough-hewn peasant red suitable primarily for blending into generic jug wines.

Nonetheless, when Sutter Home released its 1968 Amador County Zinfandel in 1971, it became an instant success.

"It was the best wine I had ever made," Bob remembers. "It put us on the map, a small map perhaps, but a fine-wine map."

It was also, for Bob, a psychological milestone, confirmation that he had come of age as a winemaker and could produce wines the equal of those vinified by his famous compatriots in Napa Valley. Further, it bred in him a radical idea: Sutter Home should become a Zinfandel-only winery. Mario went along, but he maintained his frugal sensibilities. It was good to make good wine, but a business is a business.

In 1971, Bob wanted to sell the 1968 red Zinfandel for $3 a bottle. "But that seemed ridiculous since we sold gallons for $1.50. My dad said we should sell it for $2.50 a bottle. We compromised at $2.75. I have to say that for an old-world type, my dad was a pretty reasonable guy. The wine was really good, but I had only a limited supply. So I took a case and gave it to my dad and said, 'Dad, put this away and save it. Stick it in your closet. It will only get better with age.' "

Before long, word spread about how good Bob's red zin was, and people drove in from San Francisco to buy it. "One day, a guy walks in and pleads for a case of the stuff. We searched the tasting room and winery, and we literally had only one bottle left. But the guy was insistent. So what does Dad do? He took the case I had given him and sold it to the guy," Bob says, throwing his hands in the air. "He just couldn't miss that sale! I said, 'Dad, how could you do that?' All he said was 'You never know what tomorrow will bring. Make the best of today.' That's how he was."

6

The Fortuitous Accident

Mario Trinchero wasn't crazy about his son's idea for changing Sutter Home into a Zinfandel-only winery, for it meant eliminating all the wines Sutter Home had produced for years in favor of an untested variety few people even knew about.

"He was very resistant at first," recalls Vera Trinchero Torres, "but he finally reached an agreement with Bob: Bob could eliminate wines, but only if he first replaced their case sales with case sales of Zinfandel."

Armed with a mandate for change, Bob increased production of the Deaver Ranch Zinfandel, which attracted an ever-growing fan club. (The wine sold in the San Francisco Bay Area for $2.75 a bottle.) At the same time, other coastal California wineries—notably, Ridge and Mayacamas—began to vinify Amador County Zinfandel, and a competition of sorts emerged to see who could produce the biggest, most intense wine from Amador's old vines.

"We were all trying to out-zin each other," Bob Trinchero says.

OEIL DE PERDRIX

Darrell Corti was also involved in Bob's Zinfandel. "We worked very closely together back then," Bob recalls. "Darrell actually bought barrels for me. They were high-quality Nevers barrels, from the forest of Nevers in France. In return, I sold him wine at a discount to make up for the cost of the barrels." The new barrels enhanced Bob's wines, and, most important, they didn't have the bacterial taint of the original Sutter Home barrels.

Corti regularly came in after harvest to taste all the new wines. "We'd go through the cellar and taste this and that," Bob describes. "Of course, we were most interested in the red Zinfandel. This was '72, and I already had four vintages of Amador County Deaver Vineyard Zinfandel.

"Darrell, I tried something new with the '72," Bob tells him. "I took some of the free run out and concentrated the flavors of the zin."

Corti tasted the wine. "This is great," he agreed. "The 1972 is really good."

Bob's approach in 1972 was to draw off some of the free run juice right after crushing the grapes but prior to fermentation. Long employed by French vintners, this technique—called *saignée* by the French—intensifies red wine color, body, and flavor by decreasing the amount of juice relative to the amount of skins. The juice and pulp of even red grapes is white; it's the skins that impart color and tannin to a red wine.

The method worked beautifully—the 1972 Sutter Home Zinfandel was a marvelously dark, rich wine. But Bob had a small puzzle on his hands. "I've got these 11 barrels of the white juice that I fermented separately, and I don't know what to do with them."

He considered dumping it into a big blend of Chablis. "We still had jugs of Chablis back then." But Corti suggested they taste it first. "I didn't particularly care for it," remembers Bob. "It was hard, and it was white, and it was dry, and it was coarse. It tasted kind of like a coarse Chardonnay. But Darrell said, "Hmmm, this is kind of interesting. Maybe we can find a niche market for it."

"Darrell said, 'You know what? Bottle it up and I'll buy half of it.' I thought this was great. You're talking about 220 cases total, so if he buys 110 cases, it would help me out. Naturally, I agreed."

The next question was, of course, what to call the wine. Corti told Bob there was a wine in France called *Oeil-de-Perdrix* ("Eye of the Partridge") a white wine made from the Pinot Noir grape. True *Oeil-de-Perdrix* has a slight pink tinge. (Note that the French original was hyphenated, whereas the Sutter Home version was not.)

"Mine didn't have that color until later," notes Bob. "But that's what we decided to call the first vintage." Roger and Bob made up the plain white label, with just the name *Oeil de Perdrix* on it, and sent it off to the Bureau of Alcohol, Tobacco and Firearms. BATF quarreled with the wording. "They said a wine label can't use solely a foreign term," Bob explains. "You have to include some sort of an English-language descriptive. 'It's white, and it's Zinfandel,' I thought. So underneath *Oeil de Perdrix,* I wrote 'White Zinfandel.' And they approved it."

Bob affixed the labels to the bottles, but the wine did not meet with instant acceptance. The initial production from the 1972 vintage sold mainly in the winery tasting room, and most who sampled it found the novel wine dry and austere. "Plus, the wine was hard to sell. I mean, when you went into a store where would you put it? It's not really a white wine because it's a Zinfandel, and it's not really a red wine because it's white.

"So, in '73, I didn't make any. I also needed all the red I could get. Well, it turned out that the '73 was a lighter wine." Bob realized he had erred by not drawing off some of the 1973 juice from the skins to increase the wine's color and flavor. "In 1974, I again bled some of the juice off. It worked beautifully, just like the '72 had. With this Zinfandel, we were back into the good graces of the wine geeks and cork sniffers." But the 1974 White Zinfandel, produced in the same style as the 1972 batch, generated only a tepid response.

SERENDIPITY

Once again, in 1975, Bob repeated the process—only this time, what he alternately calls "serendipity" or "a fortuitous accident" occurred. That year, the White Zinfandel suffered a stuck fermentation—that is, the fermentation stalled before all the grape sugar could be converted to alcohol. Despite his best efforts, Bob could not get the wine to complete the process, so he bottled it as it was, with about 2 percent residual sugar and a tinge of pink color.

As Bob explains the event in his own words, "Now we're making more red, so I have more white. I made about a thousand gallons, about twice as much as I had the first time. And it was kind of funny, because that's when I got a stuck fermentation. A stuck fermentation means that, for whatever reason—maybe it runs out of nutrients or the fermentation gets a little too warm—the yeast dies off, and it stops fermenting before all the sugar is converted into alcohol.

"Remember, this white stuff is not a priority; red Zinfandel is the priority. So I bunged the white up and decided to come back later to check it out. Two weeks later, we came back. I took a sample and it was light pink. Just a very light pink. Well, that's pretty, I thought. Then I tasted it, and it was just a little sweet, because the sugar stopped fermenting. And we thought, no one's going to notice. So we took *Oeil de Perdrix* off and just went with 'White Zinfandel.' We made up a different label, and, oh boy, we never looked back."

The subtle change in the White Zinfandel's taste and appearance seemed to transform his customers' opinion of the wine. Suddenly, they asked for it, first buying bottles, then cases. Since Bob had dropped the name *Oeil de Perdrix* with the 1975 vintage, his customers now had a wine whose taste they liked with a name they could pronounce. Before long, White Zinfandel was the first wine Sutter Home ran out of each year.

"People kept coming back, saying, 'You've got to make more of that, you've got to make more of that," recalls Roger Trinchero, who returned in 1972 from college and a tour of duty in Vietnam to take a job at the winery. "We sat around, sort of scratching our heads, wondering what was going on. We weren't the brightest guys in the world, but it was evident that maybe we should make more White Zinfandel."

That they did. Although other vintners may have experimented with making white wine from Zinfandel, Sutter Home became the first California winery to produce a commercial White Zinfandel. By the end of the decade, Bob Trinchero's fantasy of transforming Sutter Home into a Zinfandel-only winery came true. The Trincheros produced nearly 50,000 cases of wine, more than half of it White Zinfandel, and were poised to begin, in the 1980s, what would prove to be a very wild ride.

WINES OF THE 1980s

By the time White Zinfandel became popular in the early 1980s, Sutter Home had become a totally different winery. The California wine industry also evolved dramatically. During the white wine boom of the 1980s, the immense popularity of White Zinfandel created a home for grapes that otherwise would have had no market, rescuing many old Zinfandel vineyards that would surely have been ripped out to make way for, at the time, more popular varieties. Today, those vineyards produce some of California's finest red wines.

Other wine styles also emerged, and the Trincheros weren't the only California vintners to profit from a stuck fermentation. Darrell Corti recalls that the 1983 Kendall-Jackson Chardonnay became that now-famous winery's major success. "Jess Jackson had opened a winery in Lake County," Corti says "and the wines were to be called Chateau du Lac. In 1983, everyone in California suffered stuck fermentations. So Jess's winemaker, Jed Steele, calls me up and says, 'What can I do with this? My Chardonnays are all stuck. There's 2 percent sugar.' Well, I said, have you tried this? 'Yes.' Have you tried that? 'Yes.' I said, look, why don't you simply not worry about it? Sterile-bottle them and sell them as they are. When these wines came out in 1984, that was the beginning of Kendall-Jackson's empire."

The company sold the first vintage, originally planned to be the secondary label of Chateau du Lac, under the name Kendall-Jackson, combining the last name of Jess Jackson's then-wife and his last name. "These Chardonnays just took off," emphasizes Corti, "because no one else had a Chardonnay with acidity and a little bit of sweetness. Everyone else who made Chardonnay made Chardonnay canonically—it was meant to be a dry wine, so they made it dry."

That is, until the accident of a stuck fermentation serendipitously blessed the Jackson family winery as it had the Trincheros. Today, Kendall-Jackson's Vintner's Reserve is the top-selling Chardonnay in the United States, and, as with the Trincheros, the winery remains in family hands.

The American sweet tooth rapidly created a prosperous new market for winemakers.

7

Boom

On February 3, 1981, Mario Trinchero celebrated his eighty-second birthday at his daughter Vera's house. Shortly thereafter, doctors diagnosed him with pancreatic cancer. After two weeks of chemotherapy treatments, he left the hospital, but, within several days, developed a cold and was readmitted. On March 28, 1981, Mario died of complications arising from pneumonia, which likely resulted from a weakened immune system caused by chemotherapy. His widow, Mary, died on November 10, 1999 of congestive heart failure. She was 88.

REMEMBERING MARIO

Not surprisingly for the times, Mario smoked cigarettes almost his entire life. Cancer apparently started in his pancreas and eventually spread to his liver and lungs. "My dad would cough so hard, he'd pass out," Bob says of Mario in his final years. "He tried to quit, time after time, but was just never able to do it." Like their father, Bob and Roger smoked cigarettes at some point in their lives. Both have since quit—many times. "I've quit for anywhere from 20 minutes to six years," says Bob, today a nonsmoker who follows a rigid Pritikin diet. "Can you believe I gave up smoking for six years and then went back to it? Insane."

When Mario died, both the family and the employees deeply felt the loss. "Everyone was hurting then," describes Greg Godwin-Austen, an employee since 1976. "The family had a reception after the funeral, but the only ones to go to the cemetery were the family themselves. People joked, trying to make light of things to relieve the sorrow, but it was sad for all of us."

The day of Mario's funeral was the only time the Trincheros ever closed the winery tasting room. "Our dad would even open up on Christmas Day," Roger recalls. "We told him, 'Pa, don't open the tasting room. It's Christmas Day!' but he opened up anyway—until lunch. At noon, he walks in and says, 'See, I made $40 today!' shaking the bills in front of us. He couldn't stand to miss one opportunity for a sale."

On the day of his funeral, Mario might have been shocked. "He probably would have died if he wasn't already dead," quips Bob. "I can hear him now, 'You closed up the winery *and* the tasting room—and you *paid* everybody?!' " Everyone from Roger to the nephews to the senior employees still laugh at the truth in this. That's the way Mario was.

Mario's death devastated his family and Sutter Home. But, long before, he had transferred control of the winery to his children, whom he empowered to make the changes they felt necessary to move Sutter Home forward.

"For an old-world Italian, my dad was very liberal," Bob Trinchero says. "Early on, when we wanted to change things, even though he argued with us at first, he let us do what we wanted if it made even halfway sense, because he knew one day we would run the winery."

"He lived to see the positive results of some of the decisions we made," adds Roger Trinchero, "and that helped him to give up control and allow us to do the things we wanted to do. In the year or two before he died, Dad saw the winery start to change from a small, local, mom-and-pop operation into a national brand—he saw us finally become successful.

"One of my fondest memories was during the 1980 crush. Bob and I unloaded grapes, and my parents' house was right there next to the crusher. I remember Dad and Mom sitting outside on their lawn chairs—they drank martinis—and watching their sons crush grapes. I could tell they had a very rewarding feeling about it."

Vera also recalls a time when Mario seemed pleased with their success, but with his characteristic sense of humor. "This was in the days when I came down to the winery once a week to do the correspondence. Roger, Bob, and Dad were always in the office by the time I arrived. This day, as I walked in, Bob said, 'You know, Dad, we really should make Roger a vice president. It's time.' And Dad said, 'But *you're* the vice president.' And Bob replied, 'Well, I'm thinking of being president, and you can be chairman of the board, okay?' Just then I walk in and Dad yells 'Vera! Who's higher—president or chairman of the board?' I said, 'Chairman of the board, Pop.' Dad stopped a moment. 'Okay, Bob, you can be president!'

"Later, when we got the new business cards made, Dad didn't want them. He had a box and a half of the old ones. Dad was not cheap, but he was frugal. Sometimes we'd see him at his desk with a black marker; he'd blacken out the word *President* and print *Chairman* in its place. He wouldn't let us get him new cards. 'No!' he insisted, 'these cards are perfectly good!' " That's the way Mario was.

RAMPING UP

Unfortunately, Mario died before White Zinfandel became a full-fledged phenomenon. Between 1981 and 1986 alone, Sutter Home's production of the light, fruity, pink wine grew exponentially, from 25,000 to 1.3 million cases, straining the capacity of the family winery to satisfy demand from across the country, fueled largely by word-of-mouth recommendations from people who discovered a wine whose taste they enjoyed.

"It was like having the reins of a runaway horse," Roger says. "Our biggest challenge was making enough wine to satisfy the market while staying within our financial means." Both Bob and he remember working 12-hour days, seven days a week, loading cases of White Zinfandel onto trucks that had queued up on Highway 29 waiting to pull into the winery. "We provided convoy discounts and freeway aging," jokes Bob.

The demands, and the profits, changed Vera's life as well. After 24 years as a legal secretary in St. Helena, she finally began working full-time at the winery in 1979. Sutter Home could finally afford to pay her. When she first started, she finished her work—preparing bills of lading, invoices, and government forms—in just a few hours. By the early 1980s, the office workload became so great, the winery hired her son Tony to help out. Bob's wife, Evalyn, replaced her mother-in-law in 1972 as the company's bookkeeper. The family part of the family business grew larger and stronger.

WHITE ZIN DEFIES CRITICS

"I can't think of a single parallel in the wine industry of the kind of growth we experienced during that period," Bob Trinchero remarks. "You have to remember, wine is an agricultural business, and changes come slowly, so our boom with White Zinfandel was really kind of extraordinary. I've been asked many times to explain it, but I really can't. It just seemed the consumer enjoyed drinking it. It tasted good. It was not intimidating. It's easy to pronounce. I guess it was just the right wine at the right time."

It's not surprising Americans found White Zinfandel attractive, for it possesses many of the qualities they find appealing in a beverage: It's light, fresh, slightly sweet, visually attractive, easy to understand, best served chilled, and enjoyable on its own or with food. For a great many, it was the first wine they really liked to drink. "I remember growing up in a small town in Arkansas," says Wendy Riley, a popular hostess at one of the valley's most acclaimed restaurants, Bouchon. Sutter Home White Zinfandel is not likely found on the wine lists of upscale restaurants, especially those in image-conscious Napa Valley, but it influenced this sparkly young woman's entry into the professional food and wine industry. "Sutter Home White Zinfandel was what people back home drank, myself included. My mom later introduced me to other wines, and I developed a liking for Chardonnay, Cabernet, and such," she says, sipping a flute of Schramsberg sparkling wine. "But until White Zinfandel came along, nobody we knew even drank wine; all they drank was beer. 'Never laugh at people because they drink White Zinfandel,' Mom said. 'Because of it, they're learning how to appreciate wine.' "

Turn a Deaf Ear

The very qualities of White Zinfandel that appealed to Riley's friends and millions of novice wine drinkers—its simplicity and accessibility—condemned it in the eyes of others, especially wine writers and other wine sophisticates both inside and outside the wine industry.

As its popularity grew, Sutter Home and the Trincheros became the target of sometimes nasty barbs characterizing White Zinfandel as soda pop (not "real" wine) and its makers as violators of a sacred, European wine-making tradition. A typical comment came from one syndicated wine writer who said, in the course of praising another wine from Sutter Home, "It's so good, it almost makes me want to forgive Sutter Home for making White Zinfandel."

"If we had listened to our critics at the time, we would never have made White Zinfandel," Roger asserts. "They told us we were bastardizing the grape. And we tried to tell them, 'Wait a minute; this is our business, and the customers, the people with the money, are saying this is what they want. We're going to make it for them; we don't care what you say.'"

"It's really quite a revolutionary theory in the wine business," adds Bob. "Normally, we try to replicate something that was created in Europe, usually in France. You know, 'My Cabernet tastes just like Bordeaux,' or 'My Pinot Noir tastes just like Burgundy.'

"White Zinfandel doesn't taste like anything in Europe; it's totally American. I think one of the reasons wine critics had trouble with it is that they like to put things in categories, in an enological and historical context. But here was a wine that had no history, no context, that was not found in Europe. So they didn't know what to do with it and decided it was a flash in the pan that would go away."

Critics didn't receive White Zinfandel well. "The reason is understandable," explains Bob with full sincerity. "When you're a wine critic, you've educated yourself to the classics of wine, and a classic wine is pretty strict on how it is made, what it's supposed to look like, taste like, and so on. There are some people who feel that even white wine should not be considered classic. A wine's first duty is to be red. Right? White wine is an oxymoron," he says with a laugh.

"So White Zinfandel flies in the face of somebody who is classically trained in wine. That's why they didn't like it. It also kind of showed their fallacy, because most of them stuck their necks out and said it's a fly-by-night thing. It's going to be gone next month. Of course, White Zinfandel just became more and more popular. So here are these people, banging around, saying this is not wine! You can't drink this! It's dying! It's like beer! Then, all of a sudden, they had to be quiet, because they were making fools of themselves. After that, they simply walked away from our White Zinfandel and just ignored it."

Did the criticisms bother Bob? "Oh, a little bit, sure," he says. "But then, I always have my financial statement to cheer me up," he replies with a wide, toothy grin.

Writers who denigrate White Zinfandel to their readers, many of whom probably drink it, equally amuse Bob. "Can you imagine a guy in a Rolls-Royce going up to a guy in a Volkswagen and saying, 'You know, you're an idiot for driving a Volkswagen?' "

More than one writer has asked Bob whether he doesn't harbor a secret desire to make the great California Cabernet. "My stock response is that I'd rather sell 4 million cases of White Zinfandel each year and go out and *buy* the great California Cabernet."

"White Zinfandel taught us a very important lesson," Roger Trinchero says, "one we have never forgotten and continue to base our philosophy of business on: Listen to the consumer; find out what they want, and give them what they want."

White Zinfandel's Serious Merits

One critic who didn't belittle Sutter Home White Zinfandel when it first came out and who still praises it is nationally syndicated wine columnist Dan Berger. Berger's opinion of Sutter Home White Zinfandel sharply deviates from the views of most wine geeks, but he bases his perspective on a very persuasive argument.

"I prefer a style of wine that is true to the grape, and not to the barrel, not to some exalted homogenization concept," he explains. "I look at the last five years as a parody of the way wine once was made, when wines more legitimately reflected the character of their region. I recognize that the Trincheros made the vast majority of their profits on White Zinfandel. But White Zinfandel is a product of 75 percent Zinfandel grapes, which truly impart the majority of the flavor. Sutter Home White Zinfandel is, in fact, quite reputable. It does have a real sense of style."

Berger is well aware that his is not the typical critic's response. "Some people might consider a vintner whose livelihood centers on a wine they view as simple as White Zinfandel is therefore not adhering to a style that existed in the past. But the fact is that White Zinfandel is likely to be more interesting than today's Chardonnay, because White Zinfandel is essentially a product of grapes and not barrels. Today's Chardonnay is a product of barrels more than it is of the Chardonnay grape. So historically, you might make the argument that Chardonnay became bastardized in a desire to homogenize flavors, in the quest for some mystical high tasting score. In spite of that, wineries are given all sorts of world acclaim for wines I consider to be utterly undrinkable. I would sooner have a glass of wine that smelled and tasted of grapes, like Sutter Home White Zinfandel, than a glass that smelled and tasted of barrels and production techniques."

Though the grapes used in Sutter Home White Zinfandel come from non–Napa Valley vineyards, Berger still respects the wine. He makes the argument that you can divide wines into two fairly even categories. The first type includes wines that speak of a place. The other type includes wines that speak of a concept.

"In Sutter Home White Zinfandel," he explains, "the Trincheros have shown a great understanding of concept, which is a perfectly legitimate way of making wines." And it's not, in Berger's opinion, limited to just white zin. "When Trinchero Family Estates puts out a varietal bottle of wine, the track record of this company is that the wine is absolutely going to carry the stamp of the varietal. It's going to smell and taste like the varietal. Now, to me, that is a truly compelling argument in behalf of the family understanding that they owe an allegiance to the style of wine that has concept—not necessarily better or worse than the wine that is true to its region.

"Now I would hope that other wineries would have, as I believe you have to have, a philosophy to be successful, though wineries without philosophy do exist. At least the Trincheros have acknowledged that, in the past 30 years, their responsibility to the concept of wine is essential to what they're making. I don't pick up a bottle of Trinchero wine without being fully aware that it is going to have varietal character, and I think that's one of their greatest claims to fame. A lot of people think the Trincheros' greatest claim to fame is the millions of cases of White Zinfandel, which continue to appeal to a broad range of people. That's certainly the case. But I don't care as much about that as the overriding philosophical approach: If the wine is going to be on the shelf with a varietal designation, it better darn well smell and taste like the varietal. That's certainly as commendable a strategy as anybody's."

Whether you agree or disagree with the merits of Sutter Home White Zinfandel, no one can deny its impact. Its rapidly escalating popularity boosted all wine sales, not just Sutter Home's, and during this boom period, the family, for the first time, brought non-family members into the business.

THE FIRST EMPLOYEES

For more than 20 years, Sutter Home was almost entirely a family affair, with only a handful of employees. Even the children helped out.

"My first recollection of working in the winery," says Tony Torres, Vera's son, "was in 1967 or '68, when I was eight or nine years old, working on the bottling line. Our job was to put the plastic seals on the gallon jugs. If we did 40 cases a day, that was a good day. In the mid-'70s we bought our first automated bottling line. It was actually this old, prehistoric line. That was one of the first cellar experiences I had, assisting on the bottling line."

The purchase of the line was just one indication that the Trincheros had made progress. They also hired their first employees. "The people working in the cellar then were Hal Huffsmith, Steve Bertolucci, and Uncle Bob," Tony recalls. "Uncle Roger was running the bottling line."

A New Winemaker

Steve Bertolucci, with a family history in the north coast wine business, was the first employee, hired in 1968 to help Bob Trinchero with wine making and anything else that needed to be done. He stayed with the company for more than 30 years before retiring.

Bertolucci was not a big man, but he was strong. His wolfish grin suggested he was not averse to some serious horseplay, yet he was a devoted family man whose wife worked at another local winery and whose son would eventually also work at Sutter Home. Bertolucci was very affable, but, if you criticized one of his wines, or anything pertaining to Sutter Home, he could turn steely in an instant. You could joke with Steve Bertolucci, but not mess with him—exactly the sort of person the Trincheros seem inclined to employ.

Tony's brother Bobby notes, "He was a hardworking guy. He had some wine-making experience, but he also learned to make wine from Uncle Bob. My Uncle Bob used to get so mad at him. He gave him his enology book, a wine-making bible. 'Steve, I want you read this,' Bob would say, and he knew Steve never even opened up the cover. But Steve had a real feel for how to make wine. He had a great nose. He didn't have a formal enology back-ground from Davis or another school. He learned from experience, which is the way my Uncle Bob learned."

Tony recalls, "He was a great guy. I remember the story of when my cousin Dave fired him." Dave, Bob's son, was nine or ten years old. "He didn't like whatever Steve was doing, so he says, 'You're fired!' Of course, Steve goes into Bob's office and says, 'Can he do that?' 'No,' Uncle Bob, says, 'get back to work.' "

Production manager Norm Krause also remembers Steve Bertolucci. "Steve grew up with Roger. They were playmates as kids, and he was a great guy. Roger and he were very good friends. He didn't have a lot of formal training, but his father had been a winemaker, and he had a great palate and an unconventional style. Really, he was just like one of the guys, which is not how you usually think of a manager. The winemaker jokes don't apply to him. He was an on-the-ground type of guy. Pulling hoses, doing whatever it took to get the grapes crushed."

The Science Guy

In 1976, Hal Huffsmith, with degrees in enology and agricultural economics, came aboard. Smart, earnest, and inquisitive, Huffsmith focused initially on lab work, production, and bottling, but then segued into vineyard management when the Trincheros began to acquire property in the mid-1980s.

"I started in '76, as an assistant winemaker to Steve Bertolucci," says Huffsmith, a tall, lean fellow with short, silver hair and an articulate but casual speaking manner. "At the time, the Trincheros owned no vineyards of their own; they were buying grapes. But in the early '80s, Bob took advantage of property values at the time and growers that were going under. Once the Trincheros owned their own vineyards, someone needed to take care of the grapes." With Huffsmith's education and experience, he naturally became the man to do it.

As an early Sutter Home employee, Huffsmith was

unique in that he had both formal education and real winery experience. Just before joining Sutter Home, he worked for Stag's Leap Winery and wasn't very happy with his job. "One day, I ran into Helene Clark, a woman who had formed a group of bottling-line women," he says. "They were workers who went around and bottled for small wineries. She told me, 'You should go work for Sutter Home. They're a lot nicer over there.' " Today, Huffsmith continues to work for the Trincheros as the company's vice president of vineyard operations.

Even before overseeing the vineyards, Huffsmith proved an important player in the Trinchero success story. "Back then, Sutter Home was a winery run by feel. I started doing the lab work—checking the alcohol content, the malolactic fermentation, and such. My real value to the company emerged when White Zinfandel started to become popular. We had to sterile-bottle it, which was not a real common concept then."

Sterile bottling may not have been necessary for other Trinchero wines, but it was extremely important in the case of White Zinfandel. "The wine was sweet. If you bottle it with yeast, the yeast will ferment and the bottle will blow its cork," explains Huffsmith. "So we had to make sure the wine making was sterile. Even a tiny amount of yeast bacteria can produce a secondary fermentation in the bottle. We made red wine, which is a very stable product, but white wines that are low in alcohol and high in sugar are very problematical if you don't get them clean when they go in the bottle. So we relied on innovations of the industry to come up with a system that allowed us to do a lot of sterile bottling without using preservative chemicals. Once we got that down, White Zinfandel did pretty well. It was a stable product, and this allowed Bob and Roger to market White Zinfandel freely and widely. They didn't have to worry about keeping it close to home or switching out bottles on the shelf after a time."

Solid Support

Greg Godwin-Austen also came aboard in 1976. Easy-going, with thinning red hair, graying beard, and a round belly more indicative of beer than wine, Godwin-Austen first worked in the tasting room, then in the cellar. He came to Sutter Home not because of a particular appreciation for wine, but because he needed to support himself while in college. "I initially came to Santa Rosa to visit a college friend. I left Colorado in February, when the snow was waist deep. Once I got here, it was beautiful. Just beautiful. So I decided to stay. I thought I'd moved to heaven." Godwin-Austen's friend had answered an ad seeking someone to work in the Sutter Home retail room. "My friend said they were looking for part-time help, too, so I applied and got a job," he recalls. "At that time in the retail room, a hundred-dollar day was a good day. Business was slow, mainly tourists and a few Bay Area customers. So most of the time I sat and worked on my schoolwork." Sutter Home wines sold for about $3 a bottle then, and White Zinfandel was in its very early days. Godwin-Austen eventually became a permanent, full-time employee. Today, he is the winery's director of special projects, vying with Hal Huffsmith for the title of longest Sutter Home employee, or perhaps more accurately, earliest family adoptee.

Even in the early days, the Trincheros treated their employees like family. As Godwin-Austen recalls, Mary would feed the whole group. He, Bertolucci, and Huffsmith would join Mario, Mary, Evalyn, Bob, and any other family members that happened to be around for lunch every day at Mario's house. "They always included us," he says.

Over the years, Godwin-Austen's loyalty to the Trincheros has not gone unnoticed. "I was unable to work for several months," explains Godwin-Austen. "The family continued to pay my salary the whole time. Bob or Roger would call me every couple of weeks to say hi, how ya doing? I can't say they would do that with all employees, but they did it with me."

GROWING PAINS

The Trincheros now had a good staff to help them make wine, but they had no in-house salespeople. In the late 1970s, Bob Trinchero became one of the first California vintners to foresee the importance of developing markets outside of California, and the family hired a national marketing company, Vintage Wine Merchants, to handle out-of-state distribution of their wines. Inside California, a team of brokers handled sales.

Sales of White Zinfandel ramped up. In one meeting, Bob and Roger enthusiastically told their reps at Vintage Wine Merchants that they planned to double production, from 15,000 to 30,000 cases. The lead salesman, John Skupny, balked. Skupny, in a *Wine Spectator* article, said that they feared the increased production would be hard to sell: "Upon the Trincheros leaving, our boss, Fred Holzknecht, got all mad, started screaming at us and told us, 'Well, you guys, the Blue Nun of California just walked out that door'" (Bullard 1994). In a parallel success story, Germany's Blue Nun was a completely different wine from Sutter Home White Zinfandel, but its sales grew rapidly in the 1960s and early 1970s. It became a huge sensation.

Realizing that Sutter Home White Zinfandel had similar potential, Vintage Wine Merchants wisely reconsidered its position on increased production.

The Trincheros stuck with the company, and in 1982, Jim Miller became Vintage Wine Merchant's national sales manager. Originally from Chicago, Miller had worked as a regional sales manager for both Souverain Winery (then owned by the Pillsbury company) and for Heublein, which owned the Beaulieu, Inglenook, and Christian Brothers brands. At Vintage Wine Merchants, Jim oversaw the national sales and marketing of prestige California brands like Chateau Montelena, Chateau St. Jean, Raymond, and Stonegate, as well as Sutter Home.

As White Zinfandel gathered steam, Miller thought Vintage Wine Merchants, with its focus on upscale, specialized brands, might be too restrictive for Sutter Home, whose phenomenal growth would require broader distribution. To profitably manage that growth, he believed, the Trincheros needed their own sales organization.

In 1984, Miller proposed to the family that he join Sutter Home as vice president of sales. The Trincheros agreed.

"When we took over our own national sales, we really began taking charge of our destiny," Roger Trinchero emphasizes. "We knew about growing grapes and making wine, but we were a little short on salesmanship, on what it really took to get into the marketplace nationally. Jim brought that to the table."

Within two years, Miller hired 10 salespeople and realigned Sutter Home's distribution, in many cases moving the brand from fine-wine houses to larger, broader-based wholesalers capable of chain store distribution. By 1987, Miller's team sold 2 million cases of Sutter Home White Zinfandel, which became the best-selling wine in America. It also spawned an army of emulative blush wines—at one time, over 125 wineries produced White Zinfandel—which became the financial salvation for many small wineries. White Zinfandel can be bottled, released, and generating revenue a scant few months after the harvest. It is the ultimate cash flow wine.

Under Miller's direction, Sutter Home's sales continued to mushroom during the 1990s, as the company rapidly boosted production of other popular varieties such as Chardonnay, Cabernet Sauvignon, Merlot, and Sauvignon Blanc. By the late 1990s, Sutter Home was selling over 7 million cases annually, and its sales force continued to expand.

This rapid growth marked the end of the Trinchero family's run as an upstart mom-and-pop winery and its introduction to the realities of global, corporate wine selling in the twenty-first century.

8

Automation and Diversification

During the late 1970s and early 1980s, as Sutter Home's White Zinfandel grew in popularity, the Trincheros repeatedly expanded the winery on Highway 29 to accommodate increased production. Three separate additions that together quadrupled production space were made to the original winery building. But it wasn't enough.

In 1983, the Trincheros purchased an old chicken ranch a mile south of the winery on (appropriately) Zinfandel Lane. Known for decades to locals as the Lambert Egg Ranch (Bob resisted the suggestions of friends to rename it Chicken Crest), the facility quickly underwent a facelift.

Chicken coops were replaced by crush pads, mechanized winepresses, and large, temperature-controlled stainless steel tanks in which to ferment and store the winery's increasing volume of White Zinfandel. A refrigerated egg storage warehouse became a red wine aging cellar, and new buildings were erected to house winery equipment and case goods. What for decades had been a tiny mom-and-pop operation became a large, modern winery.

BOBBY BUILDS FACILITIES

Vera's son, Bobby Torres, now vice president of operations, was an integral part of the winery during this period. "Prior to then, I worked in the tasting room, the cellar, the bottling line, the warehouse. My family's probably glad I finally found something I could do well," he says with a laugh. "I studied at Cal and had a degree in architecture. I never thought I'd work at the winery. I thought I was going to be Frank Lloyd Wright or something. I actually worked for an architect for a year and a half in Berkeley, designing and building houses. The last project we worked on was a huge addition on a house he owned. But he did it without a permit. The architect evicted the guy who had been living there, and the guy blew the whistle.

"The architect went down, and I was laid off in 1993, just when we bought the Zinfandel Lane ranch. It was just an old chicken ranch then. Uncle Bob said, 'I need a fermentation building designed, and a tank pad.' And I said, 'Yeah, I can do that. It's just a box, you stick some tanks in there. Nothing complicated.' And I thought that would be it. But that was just the beginning. In March 1994, I started full-time. I was 24 years old—and since then have built over a million square feet of facilities, been through 17 or 18 use permits, 30 or 35 million gallons of cooperage, warehouses, houses, offices, tasting rooms, and remodeled the Victorian inn. It's been *crazy.* Sales grew so fast in the mid-'80s that we had to physically accommodate the expanding production, our staff, our marketing departments, and other areas. So the facilities grew with them."

Tony, Bobby's brother, describes the chain of events: "Today we have a huge accounting department and a sizable HR department—which you need when you have

500 people. You start with the sales staff; then, as you grow, you start having employee issues. 'Okay, we need someone that's smarter than us, with degrees in human relations and human resources.' So you start an HR department, then you need a computer department, and you get MBAs to run your accounting department because, now, the bankers are looking at the paperwork. You hire more winemakers as opposed to just the one guy that can run all the stuff. Brand managers come in. It becomes a huge business."

TONY BOOSTS TECHNOLOGY

"After college, I came to work here in '83," Tony continues. "The winery was just taking off with white zin. Mom quit her job at the law office and worked full-time at the winery. My first day here, Uncle Bob sits me down and says, 'Here's your office.' It was basically the corner of a conference table, with a phone.

"Roger had just bought a new computer system. I had taken computer classes as a prerequisite for business school, so I thought I knew a bit. I asked him, 'What did you get?' I expected him to say an Apple or a PC. But he had gotten an Onyx, a computer tied to the cash register system and automation." College doesn't teach you everything, it seems. Tony had no experience with such a system, but he learned quickly.

"Technology definitely saved us," he notes. "We're a relatively old company, our family's had the winery for over 50 years. But we were new in the technology area. We didn't have a lot of old junk, like, say, a Gallo or a big winery from the '80s might have, with a huge mainframe. We got rid of stuff that wasn't working and put in stuff that would. Today, we've built up a pretty solid platform. Laptops, World Wide Web, web-based reporting for our sales force and internal info.

"That's where my focus grew from. The first thing you do in a business is get the books computerized. Then, from there, you see that people need word processing and spreadsheet capability. As the PC industry grew in the '80s, the winery grew."

In fact, as Steve Jobs and Steve Wozniak hacked away in a Los Altos garage, developing the revolutionary Apple I computer, the Trincheros hired Hal Huffsmith and Greg Godwin-Austen as their first few employees. As Sutter Home White Zinfandel reached the exciting sales point of 25,000 cases in 1981, IBM released its first personal computer. Over the next decade, white zin sales reached 3 million cases, and the computer industry spawned what came to be known as Silicon Valley, less than 90 miles from St. Helena. Once again, the Trincheros found themselves in the right place at the right time.

"We took full advantage of all that technology along the way," notes Tony. "Bigger, better, faster equipment. And now, cheaper equipment, to the point where the computer I have at my desk is bigger in the sense of being more powerful than the first mini-mainframe we ever had." And the computerization doesn't end with desktops or offices. Every step of the winery process is digitally recorded and tracked, from the harvested grapes to the tanks to the casks, bottling lines, casing, shipping, and distribution. During packing, machines stamp each case of wine with the exact date and time the bottles were packed, an extension of TFE's concern for quality control.

Reflecting on the past, Bobby echoes the sentiments of most everyone at the winery: "It's been a wild ride," he says. "The '80s and the '90s have been so busy for everyone here. We bought the ranch, then we bought Green Island Road, and started building the Lodi facility in the late '90s. We bought this Main Street facility in '93 and did a lot of work here. It's just been crazy.

"And what qualifications do we have? One thing my Uncle Bob told me last year. He said 'Bobby, you know how big we are now?' 'No, Uncle Bob. How big are we?' 'We're so big that we wouldn't hire ourselves—we'd never get a job at a place like this.' "

MORE VINES, MORE WINES

Despite the enormous success of White Zinfandel, which grew to 75 percent of Sutter Home's total production (the balance being red Zinfandel and a small amount of Muscat, produced by the family since the 1950s), the Trincheros chose not to put all their eggs in one basket. If White Zinfandel were to prove a short-lived phenomenon, as critics prophesied, a more diverse portfolio of wines might cushion the blow.

For the 35 years following their purchase of Sutter Home, the Trincheros owned no vineyard land. With so few wineries in Napa Valley and little consumer demand for wine, grapes had always been plentiful and cheap. In addition, the family lacked the requisite capital to become landowners.

When sales of their White Zinfandel grew exponentially during the early 1980s and the family decided to once again diversify their product line, a search for vineyard acreage began.

In 1984, the Trincheros made their first purchase—two parcels totaling 300 acres in Lake County, a historic viticultural region northeast of Napa Valley. Planted to grow

Cabernet Sauvignon, Sauvignon Blanc, and Chenin Blanc, these vineyards provided the foundation for Sutter Home to introduce two years later a range of varietal wines to complement red and White Zinfandel.

In 1985, to secure additional supplies of Zinfandel grapes for White Zinfandel production, the family acquired a 640-acre vineyard in Glenn County in the upper Sacramento Valley. This was followed, in 1988, by the purchase of 1,200 acres of bare land in Colusa County, further south in the Sacramento Valley, and planted entirely with Zinfandel for white zin production.

The Trincheros knew they needn't invest in expensive coastal property in order to produce quality White Zinfandel, which sells for a modest price. In fact, warmer inland valley vineyards were ideal because grapes for White Zinfandel are picked early in the season—from late July to early August—at low sugar levels. A long, cool growing season, while recommended for grapes like Chardonnay and Cabernet Sauvignon, is unnecessary for White Zinfandel—early ripening is the key. The flat, fertile land of the Sacramento Valley also fostered healthy crop yields, appropriate for a delicately flavored wine like White Zinfandel, and facilitated mechanical harvesting, further reducing cultivation costs.

PRODUCT LINES EXPAND

As White Zinfandel production and sales surged in the second half of the decade, again doubling between 1986 and 1989 to 2.7 million cases, Sutter Home's production of other varietal wines grew correspondingly. From a base of 22,000 cases (mainly red Zinfandel) in 1981, non–White Zinfandel sales soared to 300,000 cases in 1986 (with the introduction of Cabernet Sauvignon, Sauvignon Blanc, and Chenin Blanc) and to nearly 1 million cases by the end of the decade.

Chardonnay Joins the Family

By 1989, there was only one deficiency in Sutter Home's portfolio: the absence of Chardonnay. During the 1970s and 1980s, Chardonnay replaced generic Chablis as the white wine of choice among a new generation of variety-conscious wine drinkers. As a result, before a plethora of new plantings came on line beginning in the late 1980s, the Trincheros were unable to secure a supply of grapes sufficient to support a national rollout of Sutter Home Chardonnay.

Finally, in 1989, the winery released enough Chardonnay to satisfy the demands of its distributors nationwide. That year, the Trincheros also purchased another 600 acres of bare land, this time in the cooler delta region of Sacramento County, which they planted primarily with Chardonnay. On September 1, 1990, Sutter Home released its first Chardonnay to market. This was a wine industry event of sufficient importance to warrant a feature article on the front page of the *New York Times* business section. Beginning the 1980s as a small family vintner producing less than 50,000 cases of wine annually, Sutter Home ended the decade with a production level of 4 million cases and became the fastest-growing winery in California and, arguably, the wine industry success story of the decade.

New products and packaging emerged at a rapid clip. Sutter Home became a top seller of Merlot, the hottest varietal in the United States, after only a few years on the market, and later introduced a Merlot Rosé, and magnums of Chenin Blanc and Moscato.

The Soléo Surge

Another innovation followed in 1991. The Trincheros knew that millions of Americans were devoted customers of White Zinfandel. But where would these white zin drinkers go as their palates developed and became receptive to more assertively flavored wines?

By this time, information linking moderate red wine consumption to a reduced risk of cardiovascular disease passed from medical and industry circles into the mainstream media. Yet winery research indicated that most Americans found the taste of red wine too heavy and astringent, which explained the overwhelming market dominance of white and blush wines.

Consequently, the Trincheros decided to develop a red wine that would appeal to white wine drinkers. The result was Soléo, a light, fruity, chillable blend of Zinfandel, Barbera, Pinot Noir, and Napa Gamay. Introduced in six test markets in the summer of 1991, the wine appeared nationally in January 1992 and quickly became the best-selling, Beaujolais-style red in the United States, spawning a number of "chillable red" imitations. In May 1997, the Trincheros added a white wine to the Soléo line, which helped push sales above 225,000 cases for the year.

Headache-Free Fre

Also in 1992, Sutter Home became the first major U.S. winery to reach out to non-drinkers and situational abstainers with a line of alcohol-free wines. Called Sutter Home Fre, these "grape beverages" were produced by a new de-alcoholization device developed in Australia called the *spinning cone*.

Sutter Home's Fre White Zinfandel, Chardonnay,

In the late 1940s, orchards dominated the Napa Valley landscape.

Sutter Home Winery in the early twentieth century.

Luigi Trinchero

Luigia Trinchero

Mario Trinchero was born in 1899 in Piemonte, Italy. After serving in the Italian army during World War I, he moved to New York City in 1924. In the late 1920s, Mario and other family members operated an inn and speakeasy in upstate New York.

In 1874, Swiss immigrant John Thomann founded the Napa Valley winery that would become Sutter Home.

A rendering of the wine cellar and residence of John Thomann, St. Helena, California.

The Great San Francisco Earthquake of 1906 caused widespread devastation, including the loss of 15 million gallons of wine.

Harvesting grapes in a California vineyard in the early part of the twentieth century.

Sutter Home Winery in the days preceding Prohibition.

Bottling by hand in the old days.

John A. Sutter, examining early Sutter Home wine.

The Trinchero family in 1947.

Mary and Mario Trinchero in New York City in the 1940s.

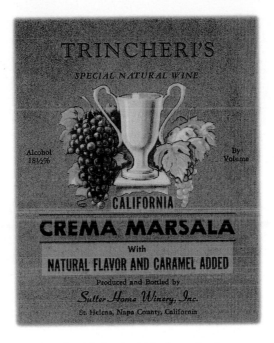

During the 1950s, the Trinchero family produced an assortment of fortified dessert wines.

The Trincheros still produce a Triple Cream.

Mario (right), Bob (center), and Bob's son, David, examine the fruits of their labor.

In the early 1970s, Sutter Home's Amador County Zinfandels, produced from nearly century-old vines grown at the Deaver Ranch, awakened wine lovers to the charms of the Zinfandel grape and the long-forgotten, historic wine region of the Sierra foothills. Soon, numerous north coast wineries were producing Amador Country Zinfandel, and the Gold Country wine industry was reborn.

Bob Trinchero checks out the color of Sutter Home Amador County Zinfandel.

Sutter Home's first White Zinfandel was called Oeil de Perdrix, French for "Eye of the Partridge." The Bureau of Alcohol, Tobacco and Firearms (BATF), which regulates the wine industry, told Bob Trinchero the name needed an English translation, so he added the words "a White Zinfandel wine."

"Sutter Home"
CALIFORNIA
Oeil de Perdrix
A WHITE ZINFANDEL WINE

Produced and Bottled By
Sutter Home Winery,
St. Helena, California
Alcohol 13% By Volume

During the 1980s, the phenomenal popularity of Sutter Home White Zinfandel catapulted a small family winery to fame and fortune.

Roger Trinchero (far right) enjoys the hard work of the grape crush during the late 1970s. After attending college and serving a tour of duty in Vietnam, Roger returned to Sutter Home in 1972.

The Trincheros new, ultrapremium Napa Valley wine brand, Trinchero, is dedicated to their father, Mario, pictured here with Roger (left) and Bob (right). Bob and Roger say their father's love of hard work and passion for the wine business have shaped their stewardship of Sutter Home and led to the success that has resulted in the creation of Trinchero.

Bob and Roger relax in front of a large oak oval cask.

Sutter Home's "Build a Better Burger" contest blazed new trails in the field of retail wine merchandising.

Bob (top) and Roger Trinchero visit their sister, Vera Trinchero
Torres.

Tony (left) and Bobby Torres, sons of Vera Trinchero Torres, enjoy a moment together in the bottling plant. Bobby, a university-trained architect, is vice president of operations. His brother Tony is vice president of administration.

Sutter Home's White
Zinfandel Gardens
include a large collection
of roses and a gazebo
with climbing vines.

Premium Red, and Sparkling Brut targeted abstainers seeking a sophisticated alternative to waters, iced tea, and soft drinks, as well as expectant mothers, designated drivers, dieters (nonalcoholic wines have less than half the calories of traditional wines), and people on medication who normally enjoy wine but are prevented temporarily from doing so. Premium White and Spumante were added to the nonalcoholic line in 1997, and Merlot a few years later.

The Trincheros invested $1 million to purchase the spinning cone column, a 13-foot stainless steel cylinder housing a series of stationery and rotary metal cones. They believed its two-stage system, which gently removed flavor essences (later restored to the de-alcoholized wine) and then removed alcohol, was superior to other alcohol-removal techniques such as steam distillation and reverse osmosis. Also called *cold filtration,* reverse osmosis may damage fragile wine aromas and flavors through overheating or the application of high pressures.

Within two years, Sutter Home Fre nearly doubled the size of the domestic nonalcoholic wine category to over 500,000 cases and garnered greater than a 60 percent share of the market. As with White Zinfandel, some in the industry scorned the concept ("Wine without alcohol is like sex without orgasm," publicly scoffed one Napa winemaker), but, true to their credo, the Trincheros again sought to address the needs of their customers and expand the consumer base for wine-grape products.

Sutter Home also innovated in the food business, producing a range of wine-flavored pasta sauces, first for sale only at the winery and later for national distribution. In the late 1990s, Sutter Home's three new sauces, all low-fat and incorporating Merlot wine as an ingredient, helped make Sutter Home the fourteenth largest pasta sauce brand and number one direct-store-delivery brand in the United

States. The company also won packaging awards for its updated Sutter Home, Montevina, Fre, Soléo and 187-milliliter four-pack designs.

One of the most important of the new brands, though, was tied to the family's fiftieth anniversary at Sutter Home in 1998. The Trinchero wines, originally named M. Trinchero after Mario, are especially important to the family and mark a new direction in the family's long history in the California wine business. But first came Montevina.

Mighty Montevina

In December 1988, 20 years after "discovering" Amador County Zinfandel, the Trinchero family made their first winery acquisition. They purchased Montevina Winery in Amador's Shenandoah Valley.

The success of Bob Trinchero's early Amador County Zinfandels resurrected the historic Sierra foothill wine industry and inspired a new generation of vintners to seek their fortunes in the foothills.

The first to arrive, in 1970, was Cary Gott, who, with his father-in-law, banker Walter Field, established Montevina ("Mountain vine") in Amador's Shenandoah Valley as the foothills' first new winery since Prohibition. Gott, whose father, Jim, was an executive with the Heublein wine company in Napa Valley, became familiar with Amador by tasting Sutter Home's early Deaver Ranch Zinfandels with Bob and Darrell Corti.

Montevina released its first wines in 1974 from the 1973 vintage and soon produced up to six different Zinfandels annually, as well as Sauvignon Blanc, Cabernet Sauvignon, and Barbera. The reds were big, bold, and alcoholic, fully expressing the ripe, intense grape flavors that Amador's warm climate fosters, and they became favorites of a growing band of foothill Zinfandel aficionados.

During the balance of the 1970s and the early 1980s, as other new wineries opened in Amador, Montevina became the Sierra foothills' flagship wine producer and among the most highly regarded of a bumper crop of new boutique wineries throughout California. Wine collectors and devotees of dramatically "big" red wines coveted Montevina's strikingly ripe, rich, and tannic Special Selection Zinfandels and Cabernets.

Right before the harvest of 1982, however, Cary Gott left Montevina after a falling-out with his father-in-law. Associate winemaker Jeffrey Meyers, whom Gott had hired a year earlier following Meyers's graduation with honors from the University of California at Davis School of Viticulture and Enology, helped guide the suddenly under-staffed winery through the crush. For the next six years, under the reign of a dispirited owner, Montevina struggled to maintain its reputation.

By 1988, Walter Field had had enough of the wine business and put the winery up for sale. The Trincheros jumped at the opportunity to gain a greater foothold in the county whose grapes had launched Sutter Home on its transformation into a modern premium winery.

The purchase, finalized in December 1988, included the winery, existing inventory, and 80 acres of vineyards. But conditions were not ideal at Montevina. New equipment was required, the inherited inventory was of mixed quality, and there was fallow land to be planted. A great deal of work needed to be done to reestablish Montevina as a top-caliber wine producer.

Making the Leap. The Trincheros saw the glass as half full rather than half empty. They had a skilled winemaker in Jeff Meyers, knew Montevina's vineyards could produce quality grapes, and they were ready to invest the capital necessary to upgrade the winery plant and equipment.

They also saw a unique opportunity to create a distinctive identity for Montevina, one that would both address a new attitude emerging among fine-wine aficionados and complement and diversify Sutter Home's wine portfolio.

In the early 1970s, Montevina had planted five acres of Barbera, a classic Italian red. Later in the decade, a few vines of each of two other Italian stalwarts were added: Sangiovese, the noble red of Tuscany, and Nebbiolo, from which the famed Piemontese reds of Barolo and Barbaresco are made. All three, especially the Barbera, produced excellent wine, not surprising given Amador's similarity in climate and topography to Italy's leading wine regions. The fact that Italian immigrants settled Amador County during the gold rush made the match even more appropriate.

At the time the Trincheros purchased Montevina, a small group of winemakers dubbed the "Rhone Rangers" made headlines in the wine press. These artisanal vintners sought out old, overlooked California vineyards in which classic varieties grown in the Rhone Valley of France (e.g., Syrah, Grenache, Mourvedre, and Cinsault) were planted, and they produced very interesting wines from them. The Rhone Ranger wines piqued interest among fine-wine retailers, restaurateurs and consumers bored with Chardonnay and Cabernet, and this attention suggested a growing receptivity among American wine lovers to alternative varieties.

Creating Amador's Alternative Reds. Given Amador's Italian heritage, their own northern Italian lineage, and the quality of the wines Montevina made from Barbera, Sangiovese, and Nebbiolo, the family decided to position Montevina on the cutting edge of what they expected might be the next trend: "Cal-Ital" wines.

Adopting the slogan "Italy in Amador," the Trincheros planted over 100 acres of Italian varieties, including, along with Barbera, Sangiovese, and Nebbiolo, less-well-known types such as Aleatico (a black Muscat variety from central Italy) and Refosco (a northeastern red). At the same time, Sutter Home vineyard managers tracked down budwood from scores of other Italian varieties and established a five-acre test and propagation vineyard on company land in the Sacramento Delta.

Beginning in 1990, well over 100 varieties, including multiple clonal selections of many, were planted in this test site. Each year, winemaker Jeff Meyers conducted test-lot fermentations of each selection. Those that consistently produced outstanding wine were planted in commercial quantities in Montevina's estate vineyard, which has grown to 400 acres and is farmed sustainably, with no or minimal use of pesticides, herbicides, and synthetic fertilizers.

The Italian collection now includes Aglianico (from Italy's southern Campania region), Freisa (from Piemonte), and Teroldego (from Trentini–Alto Adige in Italy's northeast).

Montevina is California's largest grower and producer of premium Barbera. This underrated red, when grown in the right regions and vinified properly, produces a marvelously smooth, fruity wine. (Meyers's sure touch with the grape has earned him the sobriquet "Baron of Barbera.") Montevina is also a leading producer of Pinot Grigio and Sangiovese, and makes a delicious rosé from the Nebbiolo grape. Small-lot bottlings of Refosco, Freisa, and Aglianico have drawn critical praise from wine writers and fine-wine purveyors throughout the United States.

Spurred by trade and consumer interest in soft, fruity, early-maturing reds that provide a better complement to popular Mediterranean-style cuisines than classic French reds like Cabernet Sauvignon and Merlot, over 100 California wineries now produce Cal-Ital wines, with a number of the finest from the warm, hilly precincts of Amador

County. Montevina's wines are affordable and, as a result, are poured by the glass in many leading trattoria and bistro-style restaurants around the country.

Leading with Zin.   Despite the emphasis on Cal-Ital reds, Zinfandel remains Montevina's signature wine, with over a half-dozen Amador County bottlings produced each year: a White Zinfandel, a lighter-style Sierra foothills Zinfandel, and the traditional Amador County Zinfandel, and four reserve Zinfandels. Three of these Zinfandels are vineyard-designated, bottled under the Terra d'Oro (Land of Gold) name and packaged in a tall, slender European bottle with a unique, applied ceramic label. Montevina also bottles reserve Barbera, Sangiovese, and Syrah under the Terra d'Oro label.

Montevina's production is now over 100,000 cases, much of it estate-grown red wine. The Trincheros put the historic Sierra foothill wine industry, now rejuvenated with 40 wineries, back on the map and redefined Amador County as a center for the production of alternative, world-class red wine.

9

Milestones and M. Trinchero

A s 1998 dawned, the Trinchero family celebrated, not simply because it was their fiftieth anniversary at Sutter Home, but because impressive numbers attested to the continuing growth and prosperity of their winery.

In 1996, Sutter Home recorded a 24 percent increase in sales, to 6.7 million cases, capitalizing on its first national television advertising campaign, an eye-catching new core-line package (featuring a pressure-sensitive label imitated almost immediately by a host of other wineries), and the overall strength of the premium wine market. The 1.4 million case increase by itself would have constituted the fourteenth largest winery in California.

Although the boom market for premium wine slowed in 1997, in part due to price increases by many producers in response to high demand and wine shortages, Sutter Home still recorded solid, double-digit growth, despite supply shortfalls of Chardonnay, Sauvignon Blanc, and Gewürztraminer. Total 1997 company shipments for all brands (Sutter Home, Montevina, Soléo, Fre, and Sutter Home pasta sauces) approached 8.5 million cases (over 1 million shipped in October 1997 alone), establishing Sutter Home as the fourth largest winery in the United States, trailing only behemoth Gallo, East Coast titan Canandaigua, and bag-in-the-box king Franzia.

The winery reached another milestone in mid-1997: Based on data collected by the Nielsen company, which tracks wine sales in leading supermarket chains across the United States, Sutter Home became the number one table wine brand in America, surpassing E.&J. Gallo, Carlo Rossi, Beringer, and all others. Quite an achievement for what 15 years earlier was a struggling mom-and-pop winery.

THE WINERY AS A BUSINESS

One thing the Trincheros never forgot as they grew: Making wine is, first and foremost, a business. To underscore the fact that the Trincheros are in the wine industry and not just indulging in winery romance, one needs to look at their facilities.

In most peoples' minds, the idea of a Napa Valley winery conjures up images of lush vineyards, dark cellars with aged oak barrels, and racks of bottled vintages waiting patiently to be uncorked. Such picture-postcard settings are promoted throughout Napa Valley.

The Trincheros also champion the romance of the area. Napa Valley visitors are warmly greeted in the cozy, wood-walled Trinchero tasting room, just steps away from the elegantly restored Victorian mansion, itself a Trinchero corporate symbol. But unlike some vineyards, the company does not conduct open tours of the winery itself. If it did, the scale of its operations would stun visitors. In wineries the size of Trinchero Family Estates, state-of-the-art technology rules. And as the Trincheros admit, there's nothing romantic about production.

The main Trinchero facility, referred to as Main Street, sits across the road from the tasting room, about 100 yards up State Highway 29. Passersby, peeking over the large, stone wall, get a glimpse of the lovely, landscaped grounds. But just beyond that view, the scenery shifts from a quintessential wine country atmosphere to a functional industrial setting: security guard shacks, single-story office buildings, concrete parking lots, windowless warehouses, and towering stainless steel tanks—evidence of what really goes on at a winery this size.

Some of the tanks hold up to 200,000 gallons, or 1 million bottles of wine. Overall, more than 46 million gallons of wine are stored in tanks at the winery's Main Street facility, its Zinfandel Lane facility in St. Helena, and in its new Lodi plant in the northern San Joaquin Valley.

During the crush, the whole facility emanates heady fruit aromas laced with scents of spice, honey, and flowery bouquets. A walk around the plant can set the senses reeling. But these romantic aromas can be misleading, for even in the wine business, serious industrial accidents occur. As the wine ferments in the tanks, too strong a whiff can be lethal, and even skilled professionals make tragic mistakes. In November 2002, two winery workers in Canada died. The first man leaned over a wine fermentation tank to take a sample. The fumes apparently knocked him out, and he fell in, dying almost instantly. His coworker jumped in to save him, and also died.

"These huge fermenters," explains senior vice president of production Jim Huntsinger, who is dwarfed by the lofty tanks, "are about three-quarters full, like a big froth.

Alcohol is produced, and carbon dioxide is produced. Plus, there's absolutely no air inside that tank. If you were on that catwalk up there and could put your head inside that tank, you'd be dead in three or four seconds. We have safety harnesses, lanyards, and strict rules. No one goes up without being safe and secure. In the case of the Canadian winery, the first guy went in and was dead immediately. The second guy didn't have the presence of mind to realize that. He instinctively wanted to help his buddy, but suffered the same fate."

21,000 BOTTLES OF WINE ON THE WALL

During peak season, bottling starts at 6:30 A.M. and runs until 10:00 P.M. Workers with hairnets and earplugs operate the various assembly lines, filling, corking, labeling, and boxing the wines. Sounds ranging from R2D2-like squeaks and sputters to deep mechanical roars reverberate throughout the production rooms. Despite the din, these are quiet facilities compared to less sophisticated wineries.

Trinchero Family Estates bottles its Sutter Home and other Trinchero wines in fast-paced, fully automated, state-of-the-art conditions. Even the wine barrels display two bar codes: One registers the type of barrel (its wood, age, and toasting), and the other documents the wine that's in it (the grape, the vineyard, and the date of harvest).

The cask rooms, actually vast warehouses, hold row upon row of wooden barrels stacked on racks almost as high as the ceiling. Each barrel contains 60 gallons of wine. The wooden barrels from France command a $600 to $700 price tag, while American barrels sell for half that much.

Some barrels are marked "TOASTED HEADS," meaning only the top and bottoms are toasted for flavor. Jim Huntsinger explains that, in recent years, they've managed to produce the same oak taste in stainless steel tanks by using staves, the curved pieces of wood that, when assembled, form a cask. "For the Trinity Oaks and Sutter Home wines, we hang the oak staves inside the tanks. The wine doesn't know it's not in an oak barrel, and the oak doesn't know it's inside the wine, rather than surrounding it."

Under Huntsinger, who joined the company in 1987 after experience at Christian Brothers, Korbel, and Corbett Canyon, TFE made major investments in high-tech processing equipment, including perhaps the world's largest installation of Diemme tank presses, which maximize both juice yield and quality. Other advancements include computerized filtration systems, the latest in laboratory technology to maximize quality control operations, and further acceleration of the winery's five high-speed bottling lines, already among the fastest in the world. Sutter Home now fills its 750-milliliter bottles at the rate of 400 per minute, or 2,000 cases per hour.

Computerized systems track every stage of wine making, from the grape to the bottle to the market shelf. On a good day, one where the machinery operates flawlessly and the workers are in rhythm, a phenomenal number of cases roll off the assembly line. The senior production supervisor, Norm Krause, another veteran employee of nearly 20 years, oversees the bottling line, among other duties. When it comes to filling cases, Norm proudly ticks off the numbers: 18,000 to 21,000 cases per 10-hour shift per line.

Blue banners, signed by every member of the team, herald the bottling line records: April 19, 2002—Line #1 bottled 21,279 cases of 1.5-liter Sutter Home White

Zinfandel. Another banner surpasses that record, with 21,492 cases on June 18, 2002.

Despite the desire to break records, TFE never sacrifices quality for speed. Huntsinger describes the process from the grape to the truck to the winemaker as very complex. "We closely monitor each step. Everything is done so the wine doesn't know it's in a mass market. One of Bob's mottos is to sell you a $10 bottle of wine for $5. He really wants to provide good wine to everyday people."

Trinchero Family Estates, despite its huge popularity in the mass market of American wines, is, surprisingly, just a medium-size player. "There are three big wineries," said Huntsinger in late 2002, "Gallo, Canandaigua [part of Constellation], and the Wine Group, which [together] comprise 70 percent of all the wine drunk. Wineries of our size comprise another 20 percent. Hundreds of little wineries supply the balance. There's a monstrous jump between us and the big guys. Gallo bottles 65 million cases, Canandaigua 40 million or so cases, and the Wine Group about 25 million cases, and they're adding brands to their portfolios all the time." (Canandaigua became bigger than Gallo by merging with Australian giant BRL Hardy in 2003.) "Then it jumps to us, Mondavi, and Beringer, at between 9 and 11 million cases. Only a few of us are in this range. The total market is 165 million cases or so."

Huntsinger notes that the costs of wine production can be huge, and when you factor in the variables of an agricultural product that takes three years to produce, the financial risks are sobering. This makes the scale of the current Trinchero winery, which grew from a few rustic barrels, used glass bottles, and absolutely no automation, even more impressive. "You know the best way to make a small fortune in the wine business?" asks Huntsinger, repeating the winemaker's proverb. "Start with a big fortune."

THE ULTRAPREMIUM BRAND: TRINCHERO

If there's been a downside to Sutter Home's amazing success over the past 20 years—the proliferation of its wines in supermarkets, warehouse clubs, and drugstore chains across the United States—it's that the winery may have become typecast among consumers as a producer of reliable, affordable, everyday wines. While many of its competitors established a presence in the super- and ultrapremium tiers of the premium wine market through acquisitions or the development of new brands, Sutter Home remained firmly entrenched in the so-called fighting varietal category.

During the 1990s, the Trincheros produced small quantities of excellent Amador County Zinfandel and a fine Napa Valley Reserve Cabernet Sauvignon under the Sutter Home label, yet consumers evinced only mild interest in these products, as if the association of Sutter Home with fine wine did not quite compute.

"Sutter Home has an image of value to the consumer," says Roger Trinchero, "good quality and reasonable prices. That's certainly a positive association, but it can be a negative in the sense that consumers may be reluctant to think of Sutter Home as a producer of super- and ultrapremium wines."

Image-Busting

But the Trincheros didn't let the value image of Sutter Home prevent them from entering the finer-wine categories. In 1998, as part of the commemoration of their golden anniversary in Napa Valley, the Trincheros introduced M. Trinchero, a new Napa Valley wine brand, marking their entry into the fine-wine business and serving as a tribute to their father Mario.

"It's all from Napa Valley grapes, from our vineyards mostly, and the wines are outstanding," says Bob Trinchero. They enlisted a top-notch winemaker by the name of Derek Holstein to launch the M. Trinchero program. Holstein, who began his wine-making career in 1978 and worked for Christian Brothers and Domaine Chandon, among others, was the winemaker and director of vineyard operations for Guenoc Winery in Lake County from 1987 to 1995. While Holstein was there, Guenoc won more medals at wine competitions than virtually any other California producer and became one of the most critically acclaimed wineries in the state. Bob has a talent for seeking out and hiring only the best, and Holstein was one of them.

Artisanal Craftsmanship

"We gave our winemaker one assignment: to make the best Napa Valley wines possible," explains Roger. "We gave him the resources to source the finest grapes and purchase the best equipment and barrels to make M. Trinchero wines." Holstein is no longer with TFE, but he left the family with a solidly impressive brand in M. Trinchero, which now includes three tiers: the ultrapremium Mario's Reserve Napa Valley Chardonnay and Cabernet, the Reserve Single-Vineyard Properties (RSVP) tier of single-vineyard wines from Napa Valley, and the superpremium-priced Family Selection tier of Chardonnay, Cabernet, Merlot, and Sauvignon Blanc produced from purchased coastal grapes. First released in 1998, M. Trinchero 1996 Napa Valley Chardonnay and 1995 Napa Valley Cabernet Sauvignon were produced in small quantities and targeted to upscale restaurants and fine wine shops. Their style mirrors French Burgundy and Bordeaux wines, and these and subsequent vintages were well received.

Renamed Trinchero in 2001 (restaurateurs were confused about whether to list the wines under *M* or *T*), this line of super- and ultrapremium wines receives great personal attention in every step of its creation. Bottling machines are devoted exclusively to Trinchero wines, allowing for more exact quality control. Any bottles with low fills, bad corks, or other flaws are immediately pulled from the line. They're hand labeled and hand inspected. For senior production supervisor Norm Krause, the wine is worth it, but for a man skilled in efficiency, the process is almost painfully slow, filling just 60 bottles per minute, compared to the 400 bottle per minute of other TFE wines.

Pricing Perceptions

Darrell Corti is a huge fan of the Trinchero wines, but notes they have their own hurdle to overcome. "Bob makes great Cabernet. The Trinchero Cabernet is terrific. It's very difficult to sell. Not because of the quality of the wine—it's very good. But because the price is too cheap. Wines of this caliber have got to be very, very expensive or very, very cheap." The Trinchero Mario's Reserve wines sell for around $40, considered a midrange price for ultrapremium wines. "We served it at a party for my father in 2002," notes Corti. "People said, boy, this is really terrific red wine. I said, oh yes, it's very, very good wine. Many people bought the wine after tasting it who otherwise would not have bought it."

The fickle nature of retail pricing perplexes Bob. "Some retailers advertise our Sutter Home wines for $2.99," he says in amazement. "These are wines that win lots of awards and accolades, and they're selling for just $2.99 a bottle! They're worth a lot more than that."

The disparity is explained by the fact that large retailers can purchase massive quantities of Sutter Home, get a better price from the wholesaler, cut their margins a bit, and then offer the wines for $2.99. It's great for the consumer, but, paradoxically, such bargains can have a deleterious effect on the brand's image.

White Zinfandel's affordability brought fortunes to its makers, but not without a boomerang effect. The Sutter Home brand is pigeonholed as an inexpensive label and probably always will be. But instead of laboring under the rock of Sisyphus, the Trincheros smartly abandoned the attempt to change the Sutter Home brand image. Instead, the Trincheros make better and better wines, but label them under brands with completely new images and no mention of Sutter Home on the label. As part of this effort, in 2000 the family changed the name of the company itself to Trinchero Family Estates (TFE), the parent company of all the brands, including Sutter Home, and Trinchero is now the flagship fine-wine brand.

Trinchero has developed not only fine-wine brands, but also niche brands aimed at particular audiences. For example, most consumers wouldn't recognize the company's Sycamore Lane label. "We sell it only on premise," explains Roger, meaning it's sold only to restaurants, caterers, and hotels.

Bob chimes in, "We sell 200,000 cases of Sycamore Lane just on premise. Why? Because it doesn't have the same stigma that outrageous discounts help to create. I mean, who's going to pay $20 a bottle in a hotel atmosphere when you can buy it for $2.99 down the street? So much of it is image. I wish we could get rid of all the image problems and just produce good, sound wines."

"Two Buck Chuck"

Of late, some wineries, taking advantage of a glut of grapes and bulk wine on the market, have been selling large quantities of good, sound wine for $2 a bottle in a way that actually has enhanced their image. That's how Bob's friend and colleague, Fred Franzia of Bronco Winery, made headlines in late 2002 and early 2003. Under the Charles Shaw brand name, the wines, quickly nicknamed "Two Buck Chuck," leaped off the shelves of a chain of specialty markets known as Trader Joe's. According to the industry journal, *Wine Market Report,* Charles Shaw is the fastest-growing brand in the history of American wine, and other grocery chains have rushed to create their own $2 brands. Franzia's Bronco Winery was named Winery of the Year at the Unified Wine and Grape Symposium. But the man and his wines stirred up a vat of controversy, largely because the grapes are trucked from the Central Valley to his high-speed bottling plant in Napa Valley. The bottles don't carry the Napa Valley appellation, but they do read "Cellared and bottled in Napa," which is misleading enough to cause sour grapes among winemakers who spend fortunes creating authentic Napa Valley brands.

For Franzia, the criticisms seem to fall on deaf ears. He makes a killing in the wine industry, as Bob Trinchero has done, by giving people affordable wine they enjoy drinking. And he probably doesn't care what the critics, or his Napa Valley neighbors, think.

10

Innovations and Modern Marketing

To some industry observers, Sutter Home's phenomenal success during the 1980s was a fluke, built on the inexplicable appeal of one wine destined to fade into obscurity. But the Trincheros soon proved there was more to Sutter Home than White Zinfandel and that the scions of a sleepy mom-and-pop winery could outdo business-school-trained corporate executives in the realm of product innovation.

R & D YIELDS LIGHTBULBS

True to their philosophy—determine what consumers want and give it to them—the Trincheros, during the late 1980s, conducted market and demographic research to understand consumer attitudes and concerns about wine. They discovered that the majority of American adults lived alone or in nontraditional households, and that many among this group didn't buy wine for fear of the unused portion going bad. A new mood of moderation, tougher laws to combat drunk driving, and stepped-up attacks on alcohol consumption by special-interest groups reinforced this reticence.

Single-Serve Bottles Debut

Up to that point, few wines were available in sizes smaller than the standard 750-milliliter size. Only a handful of wineries offered half bottles, and the few wines available in the 187-milliliter single-serve size were confined to airlines and packaged in ugly, squat, plastic-shield bottles derisively called "grenades."

In 1988, Roger Trinchero had a brainstorm. While his brother Bob tended to grape growing and production issues, Roger, by then Sutter Home's president and chief operating officer, focused on sales and marketing challenges, which became increasingly important as Sutter Home grew into a national brand and penetrated new venues of sale, such as supermarkets, chain restaurants, and hotels.

To appeal to those consumers reluctant to purchase and consume a 750-milliliter bottle of premium wine, Roger reasoned, why not offer Sutter Home varietals in an upscale, single-serve package incorporating the traditional Bordeaux and Burgundy bottle shapes emblematic of fine wine?

Roger approached executives of the winery's glass manufacturer, who told him that, lacking demand from other wineries, they had no interest in producing the little bottles. Roger, convinced there was a market for them, took a risk: He purchased the winery's own proprietary 187-milliliter-bottle mold and committed to a minimum run of 500,000 cases.

In April 1989, Sutter Home introduced its White Zinfandel, Cabernet Sauvignon, and Sauvignon Blanc in traditionally shaped 187-milliliter bottles. (Chardonnay, Merlot, Zinfandel, and Chenin Blanc followed.) Success was immediate, especially in restaurants, where these "classic singles," as the winery dubbed them, provided a fresh, premium alternative to generic house wines and enabled diners to pour their own glass of wine from an attractive little bottle they enjoyed handling. Sutter Home's competitors, among them Gallo, Glen Ellen, and Sebastiani, quickly followed suit, and single-serve sections became common in wineshops and liquor stores. In the early 1990s, Sutter Home packaged the small bottles in four-pack carriers with eye-catching graphics and sold over more than one million cases a year.

VinLoc Comes—and Goes

In 1993, the Trincheros took perhaps their biggest risk. Sutter Home initially refrained from offering its wines in the newly popular 1.5-liter magnum size. But Sutter Home's distributors aggressively lobbied for the move. The Trincheros agreed, but with a twist: Their magnum varietals would be sealed not with a cork, but with a proprietary screw-cap closure.

When the winery introduced its 187-milliliter single-serve package in 1989, it was with an aluminum screw cap called the Stelvin, manufactured by Pechiney, a French company that supplied many European wineries with the closure for their everyday wines. European researchers, particularly in Germany, determined conclusively that screw caps provide as good, or better, a seal for wine bottles than do corks, which can split, crumble, crack, and carry mold. Mold can interact with the chlorine solution used to bleach corks to form a chemical compound that manifests in wine as wet cardboard aroma, the dreaded phenomenon known to wine drinkers as corkiness.

As the incidence of cork taint grew in the late 1980s and early 1990s, the result of accelerating demand for cork and the concomitant premature harvesting in European forests of the bark of the cork oak tree, wineries searched for alternative closures. The best option—the screw cap—was already available.

Darrell Corti recalls the day Bob first mentioned using

screw caps on half gallons. "I said, terrific. Do it. Somebody has to do it. Because it had been about 12 years since Gallo had gone away from screw caps. In the '80s, when Gallo started to buy corks, they caused the first shortage on the international cork market. Really, you couldn't buy corks."

"They bought hundreds of millions of corks," Bob adds. "All of a sudden the strain is on. Cork trees grow only so fast, and cork suppliers tore off pieces of bark before the cork was ready."

A Closure with a Twist

The idea of replacing corks with screw caps seemed logical. However, two factors daunted most wineries: (1) the association of screw caps with downscale wines and (2) the strong and obverse association of cork with quality wines in the minds of premium-wine consumers. Although a number of premium California wine producers looked seriously at employing screw caps during this period, only Sutter Home took the leap.

The reason was convenience. The Trincheros knew that vast numbers of American households do not keep a corkscrew on hand, and that many wine drinkers—even professionals such as restaurant waitstaff—are intimidated by the physical act of extracting a cork from a bottle. Bob Trinchero points out that wine is the only mass-marketed beverage in the United States that requires its consumers to spend $5 or more for a special implement to access the product. To make wine more accessible, literally as well as figuratively, the Trincheros elected to seal their 1.5-liter bottles, introduced in 1993, with the VinLoc™, a proprietary adaptation of the Stelvin closure.

The VinLoc took the basic design of the Stelvin and added a thin saran-and-polyethylene disk to the head of the threaded aluminum cap. When applied with a pressure block to the neck of the bottle, the disk expands over the sides of the lip of the neck, creating an impermeable seal and eliminating the possibility of leakage. The Trincheros were aware they might be accused of downscaling and trying to save money on packaging (actually, the VinLoc offers little in the way of cost savings), but their single-serve package had been accepted by consumers and the trade, and they believed the VinLoc magnums would be, too. They reasoned that the VinLoc magnums offered benefits to restaurateurs—a savings of time (and anxiety) for wait-staff freed of extracting corks, simplified inventory control, and the provision of high-quality premium wine in an economical, convenient package.

"Everybody said we were crazy to put premium varietal wines in a screw-cap closure," says Roger. "All our competitors at the time had a cork in their 1.5s. But we knew people wanted convenience, so we applied that concept to the 1.5-liter size. Again, not listening to the so-called experts, but to the consumer. But over time, we realized the consumer was unwilling to break away from the cork closure, so again we listened to what they said and we went back to corks."

Screw Caps Unscrewed

Despite the many practical benefits offered by the VinLoc, the public's perception of a screw cap carried too much stigma. TFE's own research bore that out: More than 75 percent of those surveyed said they would be more likely to buy Sutter Home wine if it had a cork rather than a screw top. As a result, TFE abandoned the screw cap on its 1.5-liter bottles in 2000. Ironically, around the same time, the tony Plumpjack winery in Napa Valley made headlines for sealing its

$135-a-bottle reserve Cabernet Sauvignon not with corks, but with screw caps. "It will take more than Plumpjack to create consumer acceptance of the screw cap as a closure that is superior to cork," says Bob. "You can't convince people that screw caps are better than corks, no matter what documentation you give them. Screw caps *are* better than corks. We've shown it time and time again with the 187s."

Around the globe, a growing number of smaller wineries agreed with Bob's perspective and joined the twist-off crusade, including Oregon's WillaKenzie Estate, New Zealand's award-winning Villa Maria (as well as some two dozen other high-end New Zealand producers), and the Santa Cruz winery Bonny Doon, which even held a "Death of the Cork" mock funeral at Grand Central Station in 2002 to promote 80,000 cases of its fine wines sealed with screw caps. The eulogy was read by British wine authority Jancis Robinson.

"But," says Corti, "the biggest problem is that unless someone who is very visible—and that doesn't mean Plumpjack—does it in a big way, the screw cap won't be accepted. Personally, I was surprised when Sutter Home went back to corks."

"Frankly," admits Bob, "we reached a plateau and wanted to go beyond where we were. Costco told us, 'We won't take your screwcaps. We're upscale.' " This description may surprise some shoppers, but within their warehouse environments, Costco, Sam's Club, and other large discount chains stock imported cheeses, prosciutto, and other merchandise geared to gourmets, strategically placed within arm's reach of their wines. "They're a huge account, so we took their advice. And," Bob cheerfully admits, "we really sell more now with the corks on the 1.5s than we did before." Actually, Costco isn't just any huge account: It's the nation's number one wine retailer, selling more than $500 million worth of wine annually.

Bob notes that each time they changed the closures on their wines, though, they ran into a few consumer problems. "We had a lot of complaints with the switch to corks, mainly by our longtime customers. Why? Because they're still trying to screw the caps off and it doesn't work," Bob chuckles. "It's like the same complaints we had when we first went to screw caps, and the guy cut himself trying to pull the screwcap off with a cork puller." Bob stops talking for several seconds, still amazed. "So we had to put the word *twist* and little arrows on the cap," he says, fingering an imaginary cap in the air.

Corti is stunned. "Your customers actually did that? They shouldn't be drinking!" Bob joins the amusement, "You mean these people are drinking?! Quick! Take that liquor away from them. And this is before they even got the wine in their mouths."

Bob returns to his empathetic nature. "I guess they just thought the screw cap was the capsule, like the foil, and they tried to drive the screw through the aluminum cap. Because most people don't remove the foil. Some find it easier to go through the foil and pull the cork straight out."

At first, when Sutter Home 1.5s returned to using corks, the company received a flurry of letters. Then it quieted down and everybody got used to it. "But the ones I felt sorry for were the elderly. Some of these seniors have jar openers affixed under their cabinets. With the screw caps, you could just push the wine up under the opener, twist, and the cap would come off. With a cork puller, you still have to use your hands."

No doubt, when the public is finally ready to fully embrace the screw cap, the Trincheros will be ready and eager to deliver. Who knows? Perhaps a generation of wine-guzzling baby boomers entering the arthritic age might be the first mass buyers to readily embrace the screw cap on premium and ultrapremium wines.

Old to New: Déjà Vu

Without knowing it, Bob was ahead of his time in many ways, according to Darrell Corti. "In 1971, Sutter Home was making so much money," says Corti facetiously, "that they could afford to buy new redwood upright wine tanks, which nobody makes anymore. This was the traditional wood of California. They were very straight-grained and very tall. They went up almost two stories. They were pretty cheap. That's why people bought them."

By that time, Bob became enamored with doing traditional fermentations in wood, a practice that appears to be reemerging. "Robert Mondavi just spent $35 million putting in a wood fermenting room," jokes Corti. "At Beaulieu, they got rid of their wood uprights in 1971 and put in steel tanks. Bob jumped at the opportunity to add their old redwood uprights to Sutter Home."

"I was doing stuff then that people now consider a new discovery," says Bob. "Like *saignée,* bleeding off free-run juice before fermentation. I didn't know that what I was doing with White Zinfandel was called *saignée.* I didn't find that out until later. I said, 'Oh, that makes sense.'

"Or rack and return. That's the new thing now. When you ferment, you drain all the juice out, put it somewhere else so it's all out, then you bring it back and completely stir it up. In other words, what you're trying to do is increase the maceration as opposed to just pumping it over in the tank. You're taking the entire volume of it and dumping it as quickly as you can back into it. In the early days, I had to do that because I had no way to cool the wine. I had to haul it off to another tank to be closer to my little refrigeration unit, cool it down, and then bring it back as quickly as I could."

"Today that's called *délestage,*" adds Corti. "The Californians think the Australians invented it, because that's the way they make their wines."

"Is that the same thing as rack and return?" Bob asks, with sincerity. "Oh, I never heard it called that before." To this day, though the two men see each other only occasionally, they still share a mutual respect, and Bob is ever humble in his quest to learn from others.

Risky Business

The Trincheros have established a habit of breaking with industry convention and inviting the scorn of wine traditionalists. In doing so, they've attracted huge pools of new customers and bolstered their reputation as innovators and risk takers, a surprising turn for what had been a sleepy jug-wine-producing winery just 30 years earlier.

"Our willingness to take risks has its basis in the fact that we're family owned," says Roger Trinchero. "We don't have to answer to corporate shareholders. We look at everything in terms of where we want to be down the road, not what we want to accomplish by the end of the year. Our decision making is guided by the desire for long-term gain rather than short-term profit.

"Another reason we're more apt to take chances is that we regard the wine business as a business, not just romance. A lot of wine people get caught up in the romance and forget they're dealing with a business.

"We realized early on, with the success of White Zinfandel, that we needed to pay attention to what consumers want. So we keep our ear to the ground. All of our innovations resulted from that process. And once we make a decision to introduce a new product, we proceed very quickly to implement that decision. It's a matter of listening to the consumer and trusting our instincts."

MARKETING MAGIC

During the first half of the 1980s, the overwhelming demand for Sutter Home White Zinfandel became the Trincheros' biggest problem. The winery struggled to keep its customers supplied.

The Trincheros filled distribution channels and tapped new sales venues. As competition emerged from other large, varietal wine producers, they saw a strong need for brand-building programs. Jim Miller spent the mid-1980s putting together a sales force and national distribution network. Now he turned his attention to marketing.

His first move was to hire Alex Morgan as the winery's marketing director. Morgan was a brilliant, charismatic young man who, at age 21, had been general sales manager of Grape Empire (later sold to Southern Wine & Spirits), Sutter Home's northern California distributor. A high-energy, 300-pounder with an unmatched sense of humor, spellbinding oratorical style, and knack for clear-headed analysis and strategy, Morgan immediately created high-impact Sutter Home promotions and point-of-sale materials to attract the attention of American wine drinkers.

A fundamental change occurred in the American wine business in the late 1980s. Historically, wine in the United States was sold only in wineshops and liquor stores, and generic jug wines dominated the market. However, as affluent, well-traveled baby boomers embraced wine as their alcoholic beverage of choice and traded up from jugs to premium varietals in 750-milliliter bottles, supermarket executives realized the profit potential of offering an expanded selection of high-quality wines. Within a few years, grocery chains like Safeway, Lucky's, and Kroger greatly enlarged and upgraded their wine selections, and a major new venue of sale for wine suppliers emerged.

There remained one problem. Surveys indicated that only 10 percent of grocery shoppers passed through the wine section. If the larger wineries wanted to take full advantage of supermarket sales opportunities, they needed to break out of the wine section and gain displays in other grocery departments, such as meat, produce, frozen foods, and deli.

But managers charged with maximizing their profitability per square foot of shelf and floor space jealously guarded these departments. If a steak sauce display regularly generated a healthy profit for the meat department manager, why would he or she turn over that space to an unproven product like wine, which had no effective marketing history?

The key was to persuade store managers that Sutter Home could help them sell more of their stock products, be they meat, cheese, or fish. So Alex Morgan's nascent marketing group devised colorful materials—mass display pieces, case cards, wine racks, and bottle neckers—that depicted Sutter Home wines accompanying appetizing meals and featured items from these other grocery departments.

What little marketing wineries had done to that point— whether in advertising or via merchandising materials— usually portrayed wine with fancy foods such as poached salmon or filet mignon, but Morgan sent the message that wine could be enjoyed with the meals people typically consume on a daily basis—foods like chicken, spaghetti, pizza, and hamburgers.

Build a Better Burger

In 1990, Morgan created what was to become a landmark wine industry promotion—Build a Better Burger (BBB), a national recipe contest offering a $10,000 grand prize to the backyard chef who concocted the most creative and appetizing burger. (Today, the grand prize is worth $20,000.) Any ingredients could be employed, as long as they could be formed into a patty and fit into a bun or other bread product. (Over the years, entries have run the gamut from Southwestern trout burgers to vegetarian black bean burgers to mu shu pork burgers.) James McNair, best-selling cookbook author and St. Helena resident, took on the task of judging the burgers, and each year he brought with him a handful of famous chefs, cookbook authors, and food writers to assist in the judging.

Running from Memorial Day to Labor Day, traditionally the slowest season for wine sales, the BBB contest simultaneously accomplished a number of winery goals: attracting the attention of a large number of consumers, many of whom believed they could create a $10,000 burger; helping grocers sell more wine and other products (as contest entrants spent the summer perfecting their recipes, they bought more ground beef, hamburger buns, cheese, and other foods); and associating Sutter Home with America's favorite sandwich rather than with customarily elitist images of wine.

The results were stupendous, and the contest became an annual event that continues today. Sutter Home distributors erected thousands of snazzy Build a Better Burger displays in supermarkets throughout the United States, thus stimulating thousands of contest entries and widespread coverage by local and national food media. Most important, the winery sold thousands of cases of wine it would not otherwise have sold.

Two high-profile national food companies, Kraft and Del Monte, participated in the first BBB promotion by offering discount coupons on an assortment of their grilling-related products. Since then, cosponsors have included the Beef Council, Tabasco, the California Avocado Commission, and the U.S. Potato Board, among others. This copartnering and cross merchandising among wine and food companies or commodity boards became a model for future retail promotions conducted by Sutter Home and other large wineries like Gallo, Glen Ellen, and Mondavi. The Build a Better Burger promotion helped Sutter Home define its brand identity and positioning (i.e., the premium winery that makes wine comprehensible and accessible to the average consumer, a dominant theme in all its subsequent marketing and advertising campaigns).

"The Build a Better Burger contest embodies much more than a marketing campaign," observes wine critic Dan Berger. "It says a lot about the Trincheros themselves. How many wineries would have done a Build a Better Burger contest with the same sense of fun as the Trincheros? I can't think of any other winery that would have conceived and carried off the same contest with such a sense of style. Most of the larger wineries, ones that are trying to push their wines into upper echelons of price, are so overly concerned about their public image that they would be loath to do anything like that. I'm not suggesting they couldn't do it, but it's unlikely they would, because there's no particular down-home sense of fun, enjoyment, whatever you want to call it, at these wineries as there is with the Trincheros. Sutter Home has done it with a great degree of poise and class, with fun being the dominant factor. To me, this is a great argument for keeping wineries in family hands, because if Bob wants to do something, it's going to get done. And he and Roger have shown that in a number of ways."

By the early 1990s, Sutter Home spent millions of dollars annually on point-of-sale materials, themed promotions, and a series of print, radio, and, eventually, television advertising campaigns. Breaking with traditional wine scenarios of misty mountain vineyards, elegant meals, and upper-crust wine snobs, these programs sought to deconstruct the intimidating, special-occasion images many Americans hold about wine and to present it anew as an enjoyable, healthful, mealtime beverage adults can afford to enjoy on a daily basis, a view summed up in one of the winery's first advertising slogans: "Here's to each and every day."

Alex Morgan died in 1995 at the young age of 36, leaving behind a legacy of visionary, out-of-the-box thinking about marketing and selling wine. "Alex helped us realize that we needed to market our wines like other consumer products," says Roger Trinchero, "using colorful displays, themed promotions, and discount coupons to attract consumers and give them a reason, in store environments crowded with competitive brands, to reach for our wines.

"We also needed to become better partners with the people selling our wines. Today, we work diligently with store managers to set up shelf schematics for their wine departments to make them more profitable. And we spend more time and money—for example, with our web site—trying to educate consumers about wine. Wine marketing has become much more proactive, and that's moving the industry forward and benefiting us all."

Vine to Dine

While the Build a Better Burger contest helps court consumers and drives up supermarket sales, the Trincheros recognized a special need to directly involve the hospitality trade in their products as well, but in a way that is equally as entertaining as the burger contest.

To do so, they created the progressive Vine to Dine program, a series of workshops, tastings, and seminars held at the winery. Most events are held in the Victorian inn or at the culinary center at the Zinfandel Lane ranch. All are free, and all are by invitation only.

At the helm of the program is Barry Wiss, director of hospitality and trade education. A trim, sandy-haired man who speaks with a mellifluous New Orleans cadence, Wiss has a passion for food and wine. He's a certified sommelier and a former director of food and beverages for Sheraton Hotels.

Joining Wiss is Jeffrey Starr, the Trincheros' talented executive chef, whose articulate, genteel manner and level-headedness breach the stereotypes of professional chefs. Together, the personable team of Wiss and Starr (who resembles a youthful Ryan O'Neal) provide restaurant managers, chefs, hosts, servers, and wine buyers with a chance to really get to know what wine and food are all about. They do this through intimate wine tastings, food and wine pairings, team games, and hands-on exposure to the actual grapes and wine-making techniques.

Wiss's infectious energy revs up the attendees. His goal is to give participants the confidence they need to explain wine or make suggestions to their patrons comfortably, to remove the intimidation that even food-service professionals may have about wine. In one particular hour-long session, Wiss uses a tool he personally designed and built himself—the Aroma Wheel of Fortune™. Wiss spins the wheel, the size of a tabletop, and it lands on a yellow-colored wedge. "Caramel," he says. "Look at all the caramel flavors a wine can have." Within the wedge, spokelike labels extend: honey, butterscotch, molasses, chocolate, and more. After the session, attendees break into teams for blind tasting of wines. Those who correctly identify the most aromas win prizes. But the mere experience of tasting and learning about wines in a fun and entertaining session is the real prize for all—that and spending a complimentary week at the private Sutter Home Victorian in Napa Valley wine country.

By educating the people who interface with the wine-drinking public and who are often asked to make recommendations about wine, the Trincheros also win. Olive Garden, a national chain of Italian restaurants, regularly sends its employees through the programs. No one is required to recommend Trinchero wines as a condition of attendance, but just the fact the attendees gain confidence about wine and food is a positive step, and more than likely their Trinchero tasting experiences will leave positive, lasting impressions.

11

Why Work Anywhere Else?

"We attract good people because we're successful, and we're successful because we have good people," says Roger. "Our best decisions are the ones that bring quality people here to work for us."

Bob, Roger, and Vera treat Sutter Home employees as members of their extended family and attribute much of their success to the people who work for them.

"If I had to choose one reason we've been successful," says Bob, "and I know my brother and sister would agree with me—it's that, through luck or intuition, we chose the right people to run the different departments at the winery. Whether you're talking about sales, marketing, production, or vineyards, we have the best people. They work very hard, and we give them a free hand to exercise their talents. They do a fantastic job and are the ones who have brought us to the level we're at today."

"You know," adds Roger, "a lot of people ask me what I do here. Sometimes, I have to scratch my head to figure that out. But what I really do is enlist the expertise of the people we hire and trust them to bring me the information I need to make intelligent decisions that will positively affect the long-term interests of the winery. We're fortunate to have people who possess a passion for the business and show it. They're not averse to working a few extra hours to make sure a job gets done properly. We try to instill a family atmosphere that makes people feel we recognize their contributions. We do that with generous compensation and benefits packages and by relating to everyone who works for us as individuals deserving of respect and support."

Why are the Trincheros so loyal to their employees? Bob instantly responds, "Because they are loyal to us. They're dedicated to the success of the company. So we're dedicated to them. I mean, we're not out there picking the grapes, we're not out there doing the bottling. The last year I made wine was 1985, so I'm not even in the cellar anymore. Someone else is doing it, under the family's direction, so they have to be part of this."

A POSITIVE ENVIRONMENT

Rarely, if ever, do other wineries treat workers with the same respect as the Trincheros, say employees who have come from other wineries.

"I think traditionally there's always been a big, huge gulf between the winery owners and the people who work for them," observes Norm Krause. "The reason I really appreciate the family? I worked for a rather big winery here in the early 1980s, owned and run by a guy who is, well, quite famous, but who can be a pretty evil person. He's got this adversarial relationship with his workforce that continues today. Back then, we were in a union situation, and I was a union member. I wasn't always comfortable with that, but I ended up being the cellar master over there for a few years. The last time we went on strike, the owner and I had this huge falling out. He screamed at the top of his lungs at me, and I defended myself. That went on for about 15 minutes, and it got to be quite personal, I felt. After that scene, I thought, I don't feel comfortable working here anymore. So, when Steve Bertolucci asked me to put in an application at Sutter Home, I did.

"When I came over here, I lost $2 an hour in pay; we made about $4 an hour back in '84. I lost my union position, which provided benefits, but the other winery had become a very uncomfortable environment, and I didn't like working there.

"So I came to work for Bob, Roger, Vera, and Mary. Quite a different scene. When the day was over, you really didn't want to rush home. You'd sit around and talk about how you did things, or just talk about life. You really felt like part of the family. *They* made us feel that way, and every Friday night, we'd all end up in the tasting room, have a little glass of wine, and talk about how the week had gone.

"We felt we were growing, too. We sold more and more wine, we hired more and more people, and the money started coming in. They started giving us really good compensation. And we just felt like we were a part of something. We would be here late, particularly during harvesttime, when we worked half days, meaning we worked 12 hours, either noon to midnight or midnight to noon. You just pushed it. You didn't worry. Whatever it took to get the job done at the time, that was what counted. We worked hard not because of the money, but because that's what it took to get the job done. We doubled our production every year for a few years. And every year, it becomes more difficult to double production. You need more tanks, more equipment, and more people to do it. It was very, very exciting—a very exciting time for all of us.

"That spirit still lives here at TFE very strongly. It's like you could live next door to the people who own the winery. You feel that much at home with them. And the workers always look forward to seeing them. If Roger comes through the warehouse or the bottling hall, they'll talk about that for weeks, that Roger was here. And it's not like he's a boss you fear, like you have to behave in a special way when he's here. The Trincheros are like us. They really have an appreciation for the workers. And respect."

TFE has an extraordinary number of longtime employees. "I've been here 15 years, and in today's employee environment, 15 years is a lifetime for anybody," says 43-year-old Rob Celsi, vice president of strategic brand development. "I almost feel like I have to apologize. When I talk to other folks, they look at me strangely," says the outgoing Celsi, a fit man with blond hair, blue eyes, and irrepressible energy. "It's like, why haven't you had seven or eight jobs? You know, employees are not supposed to be loyal anymore. You're supposed to stay, learn, add to your toolbox, and then, when your toolbox is full as best it can be, move on to the next job. Because there isn't loyalty. So I'm in a different role from the widely accepted employer-employee relationship. First and foremost, the fact that I've been here so long is a testament to the way they treat their employees. For a kid who grew up in South Philly, this is a helluva way to work it out. I must have done something right in a previous life."

Uncommon Consideration

TFE vice president Jim Huntsinger lived next door to Mario's brother John as a kid, and threw snowballs with the young Trincheros their first winter in St. Helena. "They're very polite," says Huntsinger about the work habits of the people who are now his bosses. "They call me up sometimes and say, 'Can you please do this?' I want to say, it's okay, you can just tell me what do. Say, 'Do this.' But that's not the way they are." Another employer might bark orders or simply, as Huntsinger says, tell employees what to do. The Trincheros are more likely to ask, "Do you have time to do something for us?"

The family extends their consideration for others beyond their employees. Huntsinger remembers when the Zinfandel Lane ranch first began production. "The neighbors complained that too many trucks came in and out. So Bob offered to limit production on the ranch. He even wrote it into the deed. Most people would go to lawyers, but he said, no, these are my neighbors, and I want to honor them."

Mario likely instilled such consideration into his children. To this day, a former owner of a small market outside St. Helena remembers Mario's courtesy and kindness. "He used to call me up before heading out for his deliveries," the old-timer recalls. "He'd say, 'George, I'm bringing you your wine and vinegar. If you have an order waiting at Keller's Meat Market (a St. Helena fixture), I'd be happy to pick it up and bring it along.' " That's the way Mario was. That's the way his kids are today.

The Power of Names

Greg Godwin-Austen describes the extent to which the Trincheros extend their generosity to their workers. "The family has always [helped out] . . . if you have a problem, if you get in a car accident, if you need to borrow money, anything, it is not uncommon to ask for financial help. Or, if you had a family problem, they will try to help you as much as they can."

The Trincheros also go out of their way to call workers by their names. "I remember the first time I passed Bob in the hallway, shortly after I started working here," recalls Karla McKee, TFE's director of marketing information. 'Hi, Karla,' Bob said with a casual smile. 'How's it going?' I was stunned. I had no idea he knew my name."

Another employee, Nathan Chambers, who works in the tasting room, echoed the same sentiment. "We're always amazed when Bob or Roger or Vera show up in the tasting room and call us by our names when we're not wearing our name tags. It makes you feel good, that they know you're a real person. I'm not sure about this, but I heard rumors that the Trincheros keep a scrapbook of employees with their pictures in it, so they can match the names to the faces."

Chambers is almost right. The Trincheros don't paste photos into a physical scrapbook these days, but the company's human resources department maintains a database of employees, complete with the photos taken for the company ID tags.

Tony Torres (Vera's son) was instrumental in creating that database, and he recalls how it came about: "My brother Bobby and I still remember the times when all of us knew everybody by name, all the employees. Hey, Bill or Bob or Mary or John. We knew these guys by face and name; we knew their families and kids. Then, in the '80s, we really started to grow. Someone would walk by me or Bobby and we'd go, hey, someone just passed us that we don't know. I think that's what happened to Bob and Roger. All the workers knew them and would say, 'Hi, Bob. Hi, Roger,' but then our uncles would go, 'Oh, hi . . .' and exchange looks like, who was that person?

"So our payroll department took the first employee photos for the ID cards, and from that they built a book, a physical book of employees, which became hard to update.

We turned the whole process into a database and that's what we do now. You can see old employees, terminated ones, and new employees."

Bob Trinchero loves the database. He demonstrates it, swinging around to face the computer behind his desk. One click and he's pulled up the roster of bottling-line employees. "You can search by department. Quality control, hospitality, even terminated employees are all here." Before strolling into a particular department, the Trincheros may pull up the faces and names of the workers there. "When the Trincheros call someone by their name," says Norm Krause, "the whole department talks about it for weeks. It means so much to the employees that Bob or Roger or Vera would take the time and greet them as people."

Though the Trincheros rely on a computer database today, they got into the habit of calling workers by their names long before. In the early days, Roger or Bob actually met all prospective employees before hiring them. They instantly recognize employees whose service dates back 10 years or longer. Today, with more than 600 workers, their reliance on the computer makes sense. It's a practical tool, but in no way diminishes their sincere appreciation when calling a worker by name. Rarely do other corporate executives expend personal time just to make individual employees feel valued.

There's a flip side to knowing names as well. "One day, Roger went to buy some wine in the tasting room," recalls Tony Torres, "and there was a new guy there. Roger says he needs the employee discount, and the guy says, 'Well who are you?' 'Well, I'm Roger Trinchero.' 'Well, is that supposed to mean something to me?' the guy says. At that point," Tony adds, "I did talk to human resources and the folks in hospitality and said, you've got to have a little bit of orientation here, to let people know who the family is."

THE PICNIC

"The picnic is outstanding!" Bob bubbles enthusiastically as he describes the annual company picnic. He's not the only one. From the bottling-line workers to senior vice presidents, employees eagerly cite both the summer picnic and the Christmas holiday party as gestures that are typically Trinchero, but atypical at other wineries.

It's hard to tell who has more fun at the annual summer picnic, the Trincheros or their employees. Held on the grassy acres at the Zinfandel Lane ranch, the picnic is a small, private carnival that oozes with Norman Rockwell Americana. "Adults can't come alone," emphasizes Bob sternly. "They must bring a kid. If you don't have children, grab a neighbor kid. There are carnival games, and all the junk food you can eat—cotton candy, hot dogs, hamburgers. It starts at noon, and by 4:00 P.M. the kids are really dragging, and their parents are, too. It's terrific. We also have massages, horseback riding, and those games where you hit the bell to win a prize, like a stuffed animal or a hat. One year, Roger volunteered to sit in the dunk tank—no way would I do it. The line to try to sink him into the water went out the door!"

The picnic may be more fun than a barrel of wine, but there's a serious side to it as well. In true Trinchero fashion, the family issues "Good Samaritan" gift certificates to employees who selflessly perform good deeds, such as caring for accident victims. News in St. Helena, a small town of 6,000, travels quickly, and the Trincheros take it upon themselves to reward the role models of their community.

THE PARTY

The Trinchero Family Estates Christmas party isn't just any employer's Christmas party. It's an extravaganza, and the family encourages everyone to jump wholeheartedly into the spirit of the event. "It probably costs close to $100,000 to put on, plus all the labor and planning and help from the staff," describes Roger, with just as much enthusiasm in his voice as Bob has about the picnic. "It's the highlight of the year for us." Either Roger or Bob dress up as Santa during the holidays, passing out the bonus checks. "One year, they didn't even recognize me," exclaims Bob, goggle-eyed. "Can you believe it?!"

In the Trincheros' lives, the holiday party is worth far more than the costs involved. Once, after the company suffered a few financial setbacks, Bob, Roger, and their senior managers and vice presidents held a meeting to discuss ways to cut costs and shore up profits. Someone raised the idea of scaling back the Christmas party. Without a split second of hesitation, the Trinchero brothers immediately said no. The Christmas party was clearly, in their minds, untouchable. The issue was never raised again.

Without being preachy or holier-than-thou, the Trincheros operate with a fundamental sense of right and wrong, unknowingly setting an example for others. Roger tells a story about a good friend of his who has a small business in the Napa Valley.

"One year, in November, Ron calls me up and says, 'What do you do about employees who want to bring dates to your Christmas party?'

"What do you mean?" Roger asks.

"Well, I'm writing the invitations to our Christmas party. It's okay by me for the employees to bring their wives and husbands. But do I have to let the single people bring dates? It's going to cost me more money."

Roger shakes his head in disbelief. "Ron, how much more is it going to cost you?"

"About $500 or so."

"Ron, you've got to pay for the date," Roger moans. "Don't be ridiculous. It's a Christmas party. Pay for it and enjoy it."

EMPLOYEES IN NEED

Picnics and parties are fun for all, but the Trincheros care about their employees even in unpleasant situations. The company has a low termination rate. Few are actually fired. Most workers leave voluntarily, usually for personal reasons. "We had some instances early on of wrongful termination accusations. Our human resources department does an excellent job of preventing instances of wrongful terminations. We give people probably two more chances than most other companies do," Roger explains with a touch of pride and genuine concern.

Norm Krause describes the way the family deals with what other companies might deem instantly terminable situations. "The Trincheros don't meet every new employee anymore like they used to. But they do know when a person is hired or fired, who that person is, and why a person is terminated. They have final approval to make either one of those choices, hiring or firing. They can be the good broker, to step in if they think an injustice is happening. So we're always aware of what we call 'the family way.' Other organizations operate in whatever ways they do, but here we always have to keep in mind: What would Bob and Roger and Vera want? They've always been very kind and gentle with the people on the production floor, and if somebody has a problem, we'll deal with that person as best we can, as gently as we can. Because we know on the other end of it, be it three or six months later, when that person regains his or her balance, they're going to be a very grateful and very good employee. When someone goes through hard times, we stick with them. We'll take it easy on their work assignments, or we won't challenge them as much as we might some of the other people.

"If someone has a drinking or drug problem, the Trincheros will send them through a special rehab program to give them a chance to get their life together. Afterward, they come back, and they're true blue forever."

Krause is just one of many employees who commend the Trincheros for the company's substance abuse program. "The company voluntarily pays for a 28-day recovery program for any employee who wants it," notes Roger, "and it's paid off for us. We've seen numerous cases where people were able to get back on their feet and start a healthy life again."

DAY WORKERS AND DAY CARE

Day laborers looking for work once hung around the parking lot of St. Helena's Sunshine Market. It was not the ideal situation, especially in picturesque Napa Valley. The Trincheros joined forces with The Work Connection, a day-laborer work resource for both employers and employees, and volunteered office space and a location on their property as a central hiring site, open to all valley laborers and hirers. It's well organized and includes Spanish-language translators to assist both workers and employers.

Similarly, in 1992, to counter a day care shortage in St.

Helena, Bob and Evalyn Trinchero built a 130-pupil facility. The center was open to Sutter Home employees and to the entire community. In 2002, they donated the whole operation, known as St. Helena Corporate Child Care, to Pacific Union College, noted for its early childhood education programs.

Today, not only do the TFE workers and other wineries' employees drop kids off at the cheery, pink, two-story structure with grassy lawn and playground, but so do local elementary school teachers, bankers, lawyers, shopkeepers, and vineyard workers. Any member of the community is welcome. For TFE employees, the center continues to be an optional preferred child-care benefit.

BENEFITS

The Trincheros' approach to business contains a refreshing degree of naïveté. Without the educated Harvard MBAs of other companies to direct them, Bob and Roger ran the business themselves, usually figuring out what to do as they went along. By unknowingly violating sanctioned practices, they created staff loyalty that no amount of money can buy.

"As we were going from small to big," reflects Norm Krause on his early days at Sutter Home in the mid-1980s, "there was no benefit package. We got vacation time, that was it." Coming from a union position, Krause took a cut in pay and a job that paid half as much with no benefits. "We worked very hard, but the money was what it was. Yet Bob and Roger were really open to talking about wage increases, which was unbelievable to me. They would ask us how things were going, what equipment do we need, what do we need to grow bigger, what can we do to make everyone feel good and at home. And we would suggest, a little more money's good, and a benefits package. The Trincheros listened. The Trincheros also worked hard, and as soon as the money started to flow, health insurance came in; then they initiated a profit-sharing program. Bob and Roger worked to create a benefits package far, far better than what the unions had to offer. That was kind of their milestone."

Recent belt-tightening forced the Trincheros to take a harder look at employee benefits. "We used to pay 100 percent of employee health care benefits," says Roger. "But, reluctantly, we switched the program around and initiated employee co-payments. Our annual premiums went up $600,000, and so, like most other companies, we finally asked our employees to help bear the cost.

"We took a look at what other companies did. Then we came up with a better package. And, unlike other companies, we've never had a layoff," Roger notes.

Bob and Roger both seem amused by their admitted lack of formal business training. "Until last year, we automatically gave each employee an annual salary increase," Bob explains. "We looked at the annual cost-of-living increases in the Bay Area's nine surrounding counties, which was 3.2 percent, rounded it off to 4 percent, and gave that amount to all of our employees." Bob rolls his eyes, acknowledging that this was a novel approach to salary increases.

"Finally, we had to get more businesslike. We looked at what each position was worth and compared what workers in similar positions made in other companies. In some cases, we paid way more for the same job; in other cases, we were on target or slightly above the norm. So instead of giving blanket increases across the board, we raised pay rates for those positions that were lower by comparison and let the higher-scaled positions stay put."

Employee reaction to the health care co-payments and change in pay-increase policies has been mixed. "We understand their concern," says Roger, "but we need to start operating in a rational way as the large business we've become rather than as a seat-of-the-pants, small family business. We're cutting back as we need to and asking our workers to share both the rewards and the responsibility, just as we would our own family."

12

Philanthropy and Loyalties

The Trincheros' upbringing in the early days at Sutter Home, trying to make ends meet and stay afloat, probably contributed more to the development of their family and corporate values than any single event, including the boom of White Zinfandel.

On occasion, Bob strolls down the aisles of the Green Island Road warehouse, where more than 1 million cases of wine are stored. In honest amazement, he muses, "I can't believe this is all mine and my family's. It just doesn't seem real." Indeed, after more than 50 years in Napa Valley, it's only been in the past 20 years that the Trincheros have enjoyed a comfortable level of success.

Yet this is not a family that takes their good fortune lightly or always seems comfortable with it. The act of giving back to the community helps them stay connected with their roots.

Today, the Trincheros are famous for their philanthropy. Vera is especially generous, making personal donations in the thousands of dollars to national and local charities, and the company itself donates funds under her direction. When asked to describe her philanthropic efforts, she reacts almost uncomfortably. "You want a *list?!* Children are the most important. We contribute to a lot of the sports programs in Napa, St. Helena, Calistoga—football, basketball, baseball. Scouts, the Boys and Girls Clubs. We concentrate on youth and youth activities and things that will help the youth of our community, because that's the future. And I personally give to the St. Helena Boys & Girls Club, We Care Animal Rescue, St. Helena Swim Club, St. Helena Swim Pool, and St. Helena Little League. I've done that for 15 years. I send them each a check of $5,000 each year." As Vera explains, "I've sat up and sometimes been kept awake at night trying to figure out how to take it with me. I can't come up with any way, so I might as well do something with it while I'm here."

One of the most visible programs that Vera and her siblings support is the City of Hope campaign against breast cancer.

PINK CORKS

Vera's sons, Tony and Bobby Torres, recall the day they first heard that their mother had breast cancer.

"Mom's great," recounts Tony. "She never calls to chat on the phone, and she's not very technical, but voice mail she loves. One day she left us a voice mail: 'Tony, Bobby, I have to talk to you both.' I hear this and I'm thinking, oh, my God, it's not another bypass . . . but no, she said, 'I've got a lump in my breast.' "

"My mom lives life the way she wants to," Bobby adds. "When she had breast cancer, she said, 'That's it. Let's schedule it and get it over with.' So she had the operation done. Then they come in and give counseling after the surgery. For women, it's a traumatic thing, it affects your self-esteem, your body image, and everything. The doctor comes in and says to Mom, 'Here's a card to go to a women's group to talk about losing your breast.' She looks at the card and says, 'Hey, Doc, Mel Gibson stopped calling five years ago. I don't need this.' And that was it. She just moved on."

In moving on, Vera took up the battle against breast cancer with a passion, using her family's and her personal resources as her weapons.

In 2001, Sutter Home donated $100,000 to the City of Hope and distributed more than 3 million bottles of blushing White Zinfandel across retail shelves with an eye-catching look: bright pink corks emblazoned with the familiar pink ribbon symbol of breast cancer awareness and the slogan "Sutter Home for Hope." Visible behind a see-through capsule, the campaign launched in September and lasted through October, the official month of breast cancer awareness. The magnums also sported a bottle necker, explaining how consumers could get involved in the fight against breast cancer. Consumers who sent the necker back to Sutter Home received a City of Hope pink ribbon pin and information about how to do a breast self-exam. City of Hope is a cancer center (located near Los Angeles) with an international reputation for innovative breast cancer research and treatment.

"The pink cork program was an idea that came out of Sutter Home's national sponsorship of City of Hope's Walk for Hope against Breast Cancer," according to TFE's Terry Wheatley, senior vice-president of sales and marketing, in a press release. Wheatley joins Vera Trinchero in being a breast cancer survivor. "As soon as we decided to sponsor the Walk for Hope against Breast Cancer, we wanted to do as much as possible to spread the message of early detection, treatment, and hope for a cure. What better way to accomplish that than to place it right in a bottle of our wine? If our program encourages one woman to do a self-exam or have a mammogram, I consider it a success."

In fall 2002, Vera reflected on the impact of their pink cork campaign. "It was so nice last year. I'm not sure what the tally is this year. But last year, so many people actually sent money in that we raised over $10,000 in contributions from them alone, in small increments like $20 or $50. They didn't have to send in donations; they could have just mailed in for the pink pin. Some people even wrote little notes, like, 'My sister was affected. Thank you, you're doing such a great job.' So it really turned out well for everybody all the way around."

COMMUNITY VIEWS

Veteran employee Jim Huntsinger recalls a conversation in town about the Trincheros. "I bought a pickup truck once in downtown St. Helena," he says, "and the guy at the dealership said, 'Oh, yeah, you work for Sutter Home. I remember they came in one time to buy a used car and they had to get together their funds, to pool their money together, to buy the used car—a Torino.' The dealership guy chuckled. Of course, now they could buy the dealership and everything else on that side of the street." But instead of buying a car dealership or city block, the Trincheros clearly prefer to give their money to others, quietly and without fanfare.

The Grayer Shades of Giving

In 2002, Sara Cakebread, whose family owns Cakebread Cellars, wrote a column in the *Napa Valley Register,* in reaction to a controversial book titled *The Far Side of Eden,* by

James Conaway, a Washington, D.C., writer (Conaway 2002). The book focuses on the conflicts in Napa Valley between environmentalists and vintners.

The book only briefly mentions Bob Trinchero. Nonetheless, the author's derogatory depiction of Bob as a self-serving vintner sparked fire in Cakebread, who wrote, "One name that caught me by surprise in Mr. Conaway's book is that of Bob Trinchero. An odd placement for someone who, along with his brother and sister, has given so much to our community that it would be impossible for anyone to keep track. As a Highland Fling insider," she writes, referring to a charity event, "I know the Trinchero name will appear on tonight's program as a major sponsor. I look forward to the St. Helena Rotary Club's annual winter ball, hosted each year by Trinchero Family Estates. I am thankful for the day care center they funded in town because it makes commuting with a baby a little easier for my daughter's favorite teacher" (Cakebread 2002).

Outside of her editorial, Cakebread speaks even more passionately about the Trincheros. "Nobody could be further from the land-grabbing, money-hungry depiction portrayed in that book. The Trincheros are so over the top when it comes to generosity. They give to everything: the playground in St. Helena, the hospital, the dialysis machine, the day care center, the sports programs. They touch everybody. They're so incredibly generous. The locals joke that with Vera, especially, you have to rein her in. 'Everything you make you're going to give away!' they say to her.

"I haven't the slightest idea why they're so selfless and generous," muses Cakebread about the Trincheros. "They're just honest people, hard workers, who came into a windfall. Average Joes. White Zinfandel brought them to the dance. They may not be hugely sophisticated, but they're real people. And here in Napa Valley, I don't think they've ever pissed anyone off.

"Unlike the Mondavis, who donate to the symphony," adds Cakebread, "or the people who give to Copia and upper-crust charities, the Trincheros give to everyday people. They're rooted in the community. And they don't donate to attract publicity."

Apprised of Cakebread's comments, Bob points out that the Mondavis and a small group of other Napa wineries do donate to a wide range of causes and organizations. "What really bothers me are the ones that don't give anything at all," he fumes. "Okay, we put into the community, but some of these other people don't. Some make huge profits, and they're not doing anything to give back. When something gets done here, what are the names that pop up? The Mondavis, Beringer, Joe Phelps, us, and the same names are always in the top 10. Then, nothing. No other names. You own a winery here, for chrissakes. But they're not here, hardly, they're like absentee winery holders."

Humanitas

Most residents of Napa Valley, even if they don't know them personally, praise the Trincheros for their quiet generosity. Locally, they're so well respected that they've unintentionally helped inspire a fellow by the name of Judd Wallenbrock to create a nonprofit winery, Humanitas.

"The wine industry is very giving," says Wallenbrock. "The concept of Humanitas is to take this giving one step further by actually creating a brand designed to raise funds for charity. I worked for Robert Mondavi for nine years, who, in my opinion, is the most giving man in the entire industry." Wallenbrock emphasizes he has also been very inspired by the Trincheros, especially by their efforts to raise funds to fight breast cancer. "This type of 'cause marketing' can often be gimmicky," he notes, "but I believe the Trincheros have a real commitment to the cause and have very successfully raised both money and consciousness to fight breast cancer. I truly admire that sort of activism and wish more companies, not just wine companies, would pick up the gauntlet in the future. Basically, companies such as Paul Newman's Own, Sutter Home, Stonyfield Farms Yogurt, and Ben & Jerry's are my models—I hope it works!"

THE FAMILY FORTUNE

Bob, Roger, and Vera don't even think twice about giving back to community. Do their children feel the same way?

"Mario went through the Depression," says Roger, "when he didn't have two dimes to rub together. Mom had little envelopes where she saved the tips money she found in Dad's pockets, just to pay the bills. 'You never know what tomorrow's going to bring, so make the best of today,' Dad would say. It was a different mentality with them."

Talking about himself and his siblings, Bob and Vera, Roger says, "We have a little bit of that mentality. Then I look at my kids, Mario, Carlo, and Gino, and I wonder, what sense of work ethic will they have? But sometimes they give you a glimmer of hope. My oldest son, named Mario after his grandfather, is 18. He's got an old jeep that he drives; he's going off to college, and he likes these hybrid cars. What kind of an 18-year-old kid likes hybrid cars, the ones that are half electric and half gas? When I was his age, I just wanted the fastest car I could have. Anyway, he's ready to go to college, and his birthday was last month, so I said, 'You know son, I'd like to buy you a new car.' He said, 'Oh, Dad, that's way too much, I couldn't accept it.' " Roger drops his jaw, stunned by his kid's reaction. "I'm going, I don't believe this. So that gives me a glimmer of hope. I finally talked him into maybe—maybe—accepting a car as a graduation present."

Roger admits it is tough to instill the Mario-and-Mary mentality into the kids. "I think you just sit down and talk to them." But Bob is more fatalistic. "You do the best you can," Bob says, "they're products of their environments and their experiences." While both of his children have at times worked at the winery, neither embraced the business as their own career, and Bob hasn't pushed them in that direction, either. Rather, he's been supportive of their outside interests, both emotionally and financially. "My son David was just out of high school," says Bob, explaining that David, now in his thirties, had no desire to go to college. "He said, 'Nah, I don't need school.' He came to work at the winery, but after a while didn't like it. What he likes is to be outdoors and hunting. So he became a licensed hunter and guide. As a matter of fact, we have property, Spanish Valley out near Lake Berryessa, 3,000 acres, and David got approval from California Fish and Game for a Private Lands Wildlife Management Program for nongame and game wildlife development. He charges $400 to $500 a day to take folks out hunting. So he's doing a nice little business on his own."

Bob's daughter is scholastically different from her brother. Gina graduated from Stanford and followed up with a degree in enology from University of California at Davis. Like David, Gina has no long-term interest in working at the family winery, although she and her husband grow grapes in Napa for the high-end Trinchero brand, and both she and David, as well as Bobby and Tony Torres, are shareholders in a number of the Trincheros' vineyard properties.

The Torres Brothers

Vera's sons, Bobby and Tony Torres, well-liked and hard-working employees at TFE, may be the only family members of their generation to be part of the winery's future. "The nephews," as they're often called, have their own perspective on the family's trait for seemingly unrestrained generosity.

Tony jokes about his own viewpoint, "Well, I guess it's the old accountant in me. Hearing my grandfather Mario in the back of my mind going, 'They're not doing this again!' every time the checkbook comes out."

Bobby good-naturedly agrees. "Grandpa would have a heart attack if he saw some of the money we're giving to these organizations. Seriously, though, it's all for the good, and we're happy and feel very fortunate that the family and the company are in a position that we can do that, give something back to the community, especially to the kids.

"Mom tells a story," Bobby continues, "about when she worked at the law office of a guy who passed away. In his will, he wanted to be buried with his accordion. They honored his wishes, but the accordion wouldn't fit in the coffin. So the family decided, we'll cut it in half and fit it in on either side. When they cut it in half, they discovered it was filled with money. Now, my mom tells me this story, and I'm thinking . . . God, Mom's got this piano that she's really fond of. . . ." His voice trails off as a wide grin emerges. "Let's chop that thing up, I'm thinking. But anyway, she's really very generous, and so are Bob and Roger and the rest of the family—and the winery, too."

Tony reflects on Vera's generous nature. His parents were, at best, middle income. "I don't think together they ever made more than $70,000 a year. Dad was in construction;

that was seasonal depending on the weather; and Mom was in the law office. You know, when you're kids, and you ask each other 'What would you do if you had a million dollars?' When we were young, Mom said that she'd buy my dad's mother a new house to live in. Or she'd take care of grandma or other family members. Today, she's done all that. Everything she wanted to do, she's been able to do. She gives money to the church, to the after-school programs, and after taking care of her family, she now wants to take care of the community in general. And let's face it, in this day and age, philanthropy is rare. It's just something we all try to do. The schools are somewhat of a mess, the money's not there for them; the sports programs are cut from the school budgets, so she helps out with a lot of that."

PART THREE

GLOBALIZATION AND THE NEW NAPA

13

Succession or Transition?

T he year 2003 commemorates several Trinchero anniversaries—not only 55 years at Sutter Home, but 35 years of making Amador County Zinfandel, the thirtieth anniversary of Montevina, and the thirtieth anniversary of the release of Sutter Home White Zinfandel. They've also seen half a decade of steady growth with their homage to Mario, the Trinchero brand. Today, the Trinchero family focuses on new challenges. Not the least of which begs the question: What will become of the family business?

Unlike other family-owned wineries that in recent years either sold out to corporations or went public to raise investment capital, the Trincheros intend to keep Trinchero Family Estates a family affair. But this may be more difficult than it sounds.

Bob's kids aren't interested in the winery. Roger's three boys are too young, and even his oldest son Mario, who's now off to college, hasn't demonstrated a strong desire to pick up the trade. Vera's sons, Bobby and Tony, hold executive positions at TFE, but the issue of who will actually run the winery in the coming decades, including whether it will even remain a family-owned winery, is more complicated.

CONSTELLATION

"Shock waves rolled through the wine industry last week when reports surfaced that Constellation Brands is close to buying Trinchero Family Estates," reported the *St. Helena Star* on November 15, 2001. "Industry sources estimate the deal to be worth $500 million. Trinchero Family Estates, which includes Sutter Home Winery, produces 10 million cases annually and also owns approximately 6,000 acres of vineyard statewide, making it one of the 15 largest vineyard owners in the state." The article also noted that TFE was one of a dwindling number of family-owned California wineries (Ferguson 2001).

The Trincheros quickly denied the rumor, but the news had already appeared in a leading industry trade newsletter, *Wine Business Insider.* "Constellation Rumored Buying Trinchero Family Estates," ran the headline on November 8, 2001. "While equity analysts covering Constellation say such a deal would make sense" the newsletter reported, "spokespersons for both companies declined comment."

As it turns out, the rumored Constellation and TFE deal was more than just idle gossip. The two parties did engage in discussions, and though no deal was consummated, the whole affair raised questions and issues that the Trincheros and their employees still wrestle with.

Constellation's Universe

To understand the impact of the Constellation episode on TFE, it's important to become familiar with Constellation's place in the global beverage industry.

According to its company web site (March 2003): "Constellation Brands, Inc., is a leading producer and marketer of beverage alcohol brands, with a broad portfolio of wines, spirits and imported beers. The Company is the largest single-source supplier of these products in the United States, and both a major producer and independent drinks wholesaler in the United Kingdom. The company also operates a U.S.-based joint venture with the largest Australian wine producer, BRL Hardy." Well-known brands in Constellation's portfolio include Corona Extra, Pacifico, St. Pauli Girl, Black Velvet, Fleischmann's, Estancia, Simi, Blackstone, Banrock Station, Alice White, Talus, Vendange, Almaden, Arbor Mist, Stowells of Chelsea, and Blackthorn.

Before September 2000, Constellation Brands, Inc., was known as Canandaigua Brands, but the company changed its name to better reflect its scope of more than 185 products, which include beer, wine, distilled spirits, cider, and bottled water. It designated Canandaigua Wine Company as the umbrella division of its winery assets.

In 2001, the corporation was slightly smaller than it is today, but it grew rapidly through a series of strategic acquisitions. Around that time, Constellation and its Canandaigua Wines included a portfolio of some of the most recognized brands in North America—Inglenook, Paul Masson, Taylor California Cellars, Arbor Mist, Manischewitz, Dunnewood, Paul Thomas, Ste. Chapelle, Cook's sparkling wines, Wild Irish Rose, and Franciscan Estates, just to name a few.

That same year, Constellation snatched up more leading names in California wines and also expanded into Australian, Chilean, and Washington state wines. Constellation was on a buying spree. According to its pressroom web site: "Two acquisitions were made in the spring of 2001 to strengthen Constellation's popular and premium wine portfolio. Talus, Vendange, Nathanson Creek and Heritage were acquired from Turner Road Vintners. Columbia, Covey Run, and Alice White were acquired from Corus Brands and help to round out the higher margin and growing premium table wine categories, giving Canandaigua Wine Company 20 of the top 100 wine brands in the U.S. Ravenswood, the best selling premium red Zinfandel in the U.S., was acquired in July 2001, making Franciscan Estates one of the most sought after wine portfolios in the industry. Pacific Wine Partners acquired certain assets of Blackstone Winery, including the Blackstone brand and the Codera winery in Sonoma County."

The Biggest Wine Producer on Earth

The behemoth was only just beginning to feed. By the end of the first quarter of 2003, Constellation made headlines again, this time for a deal that would put it so far over the top that it became the world's largest wine producer. In March 2003, Constellation Brands initiated a merger with Australia's BRL Hardy. The result: Constellation Wines, a separate global wine business within the Constellation Group. Most significantly, the move thrust the already huge wine giant into the position of being the biggest winery in the world, tipping E.&J. Gallo off the top perch. According to Constellation chief Richard Sands, the company, with over $1.7 billion in projected sales, intends to double the company's size in the next five years (Lechmere 2003).

Trincheros Say No

Interestingly, if Constellation had bought Trinchero Family Estates in 2001, the purchase would have made it the world's largest winery. Bob and Roger are reluctant to discuss details, but say that selling the winery was something they decided they didn't want to do.

Nonetheless, Bob, Roger, and Vera are getting older, and the issue of who will run the company in the future is clearly on their minds.

"There's no one ready to move into my place," says Roger. "My nephews need another couple years of grooming . . . maybe more," he says, humorously.

Bob continues the thread, "In the future, hiring someone to run the company who's not a family member is a possibility. We're looking at a lot of things. I'm not in a hurry, so we'll see how things turn out."

A CRITIC'S VIEW

Wine columnist Dan Berger suspects there may be more to it than Bob and Roger admit. "My guess is that whatever prompted Bob and Roger to consider selling still exists. Chances are that the same financial issues are yet to be solved. There was so much smoke, there had to be fire. A sale was almost imminent."

Berger reflects on TFE's particular situation in Napa Valley. "Wineries like TFE are always going to have people knocking on their doors asking, do you want to sell? It's just a matter of acquisition. But this family has some assets that nobody else has, one of which is the waiver of the ability to bring fruit from outside into Napa Valley to process. Nobody can get that anymore. That's grandfathered in and that's not going to change. On the other side, the benefits they have to offer can be outweighed by some of the drawbacks, one of which is that the Trinchero name is yet to be readily identified by anybody as a super-premium brand. And beyond that you have some baggage issues that need to be dealt with. I think if the next generation of Trincheros takes stock of what those assets are and strengthens those assets and tries to develop a better public image for a higher-quality product, it's possible to avoid the necessity of selling out.

"The pressures of business are not going to go away. I think the family has definitely reached the point where they're going to make some strategy decisions that will affect the company long term. Part of that is just in the realm of year-to-year operations, such things as loans and financial support from the lending institutions. And so much depends on the conditions of the marketplace. Pressures from overseas are certainly not going to diminish."

EMPLOYEES' VIEWS

Bob and Roger may act like the Constellation episode was insignificant, but at the time, their employees read about it in the trade publications, heard rumors around town, and had to cope with the idea of the company being sold.

"It was like your parents are fighting and you're afraid they're going to break up. I'm 55 years old. That was very frightening and very tense," says veteran employee Norm Krause. "When we all thought about the Constellation deal, we all said, 'Good for the Trincheros.' We were deathly afraid of what might happen, and none of us wanted to work anywhere else, but no one would begrudge them for taking the big paycheck."

Bob says the employees will always be a factor in any decision the family makes about the future of the company, and perhaps that became part of the deal killer. "We would never sell the winery and have it disbanded without some good compensation for our employees. That wouldn't be right. In other words, we wouldn't just walk away without at least some guarantees and money for them."

NEPHEWS' VIEWS

"The Constellation experience was probably a good process for this family to go through," says Bobby Torres. "It opened our eyes to some things. When everything's doing great and the money's coming in, you don't think about, are we operating efficiently? Do we have too many assets that drain from the bottom line? Are we really looking introspectively at all our departments. Who's there? What are they doing? Do we really need them? Constellation ignited these types of questions."

The state of the economy also caused the Trincheros to take stock of their business. "With all the things that have happened, Enron and corporate scandals, 9/11, there's this panic mode attitude in the lending industry," says Bobby. "Because the wine industry has always been cyclical, whether it's the grape supply, shortage, sales, economy, and so forth, we've been pretty impervious to it. But with 9/11 and the economy headed south, 2002 was one of the first years we didn't have a significant increase. Our sales stayed steady, which is fine, but they didn't hit the number we projected, for all those different reasons. We built a big facility in Lodi, which we hoped to get running that year. We have over 20 million gallons of cooperage there, for crushing and blending and filtering. In 2002, we planned to spend $25 million on it.

❧

"When 9/11 happened, we said, you know what? We're not going to do that. All our big capital projects, promotions, hiring, all those things, we're freezing. As far as raises go, we're putting our salaries in line with the marketplace.

We're taking a look at our assets. Do we need them? How much do they cost us?

"We look at this as a business. We get more involved in the day-to-day operations of some of our bigger departments. Because the last thing you want to do as a family is lose touch with what the hell's going on. We have some great people heading our departments—the VPs. They're the best in the industry, or some of the best, at what they do, but at the same time we need to know what the heck they're doing. There needs to be accountability.

"So this whole Constellation thing was a good exercise for us," Tony continues. "It really was. We're going to get more involved in the decisions that are made. Which is only right. Managers will have to justify their budgets, their marketing budgets, their advertising budgets, their capital improvements budgets, all that stuff. Hiring people. It's not going to change overnight. It's an ongoing thing. We've got a lot of people who think along the same lines we do."

What's in the Stars

The conversation segues to where the company will be 10 years from now. Will Bob and Roger still be involved, or will Tony and Bobby be running Trinchero Family Estates? After a long, thoughtful silence, the nephews respond.

"It's a difficult thing for me to come to grips with," acknowledges Bobby. "I would love to step in for Roger or Bob. But there's a flip side to the coin. I know both Tony and I could run this winery. I know we're both capable of doing that. . . ."

". . . But what we're missing are those two guys," finishes Tony, "with their unique personalities. Let's face it, when folks look at Sutter Home, they look at those two. They know us as the nephews. And, yeah, we've been to sales meetings, and obviously all the salespeople know us—especially when I get on them about their expense reports or deal with them on computer stuff. They know me. But are we as charismatic as those two? Bob and Roger are very natural speakers, very self-effacing. I think most of the family is, and I think we've inherited some of that. But are we ready to step in? Bob was 43 and was doing all sorts of stuff before I even came into the winery."

"And they already learned a lot of this along the way," notes Bobby. "I think I'm capable of doing it, running the company, and I think Tony's capable. This business is just based on relationships—whoever the customer is, whether it's the distributor, the retailer, or in the tasting room. You sit down, talk to them, get to know them. Am I going to become Bob Trinchero? No. Am I going to become Roger? No. But still I represent the family. Tony can do it, too."

Bobby, in a tender, honest way, adds "The big thing I want to say is, the tough thing for me—and Roger has let me know what kind of commitment is required for a winery like this—is being away from your family. I have two kids, one was nine in December and the other is seven. Roger told me, with his kids, he missed a lot of their lives—baseball, sports games, Christmas shows, just being there. Because he was on the road all the time. To me, that's not very palatable. It's not something I feel comfortable with—to be gone for a week or two every month. It's a lifestyle I'm not sure I'm willing to accept. Now I'm willing to do some of that. But I don't know. . . ."

Bringing in an Outsider?

Tony brings up another possibility. "So there's always been the other talk: Would we hire someone from the outside to run the company? And that's open. We'd have to be sure they shared the same philosophy. I think the concern I have is that you would lose that family thing of having a Trinchero in charge. Even though the family's around.

"Let's face it. Everyone knows who ran the Gallo winery. Ernest and Julio. Now they've got the younger generation, the fourth generation, Matthew and Gina. They all basically filled in. Are we saying that we're holding the business in check for our kids, in the future? Roger's boys may one day be the ones to run the company, and we're gonna hold onto the whole piece of it until then. Or maybe not. We don't know. It's hard to say. I would still like to work here.

"I would also like to have a little more time off," Tony jokes. "But when I'm 56, I wouldn't want to work as hard as Roger is right now. Even though he's scaled back, there's still a lot of demand for him. You look at things and ask, 'Would I like to be president?' Maybe I'd much rather be in the background. If you're going to be in the limelight, you've got to be prepared for it.

"A lot of these distributors we work with are like us, families. We now deal with the sons and daughters, who are all our age. It's like cycles. The old guard goes out, the new guard comes in. But we still have those relationships. I still think we've got a goal to be one of the largest family-owned wineries and to try to maintain that.

Tony gazes out his office window. "We've got a wonderful lifestyle in St. Helena. It's a beautiful place to live."

14

Myth Busters and Strategies for Success

B ob proudly notes that his brother Roger is the first Trinchero (and the only one of the three siblings) to have gone to college. For the CEO and chairman of one of California's largest wineries, Bob's own lack of higher education isn't a concern.

"Would I have been better off going to college?" Bob shrugs. After all, he makes regular trips to the bank without a college degree.

Bob's an avid reader of medical books, but when asked about reading business books, he offers a long, deep "Noooo," slowly shaking his head as if to emphasize that he's made his fortune without business books or gurus to guide him, or perhaps that business books simply bore him. Indeed, his modest office contains a large, uncluttered wooden desk, two guest chairs, a couple of couches around a coffee table, and a TV. Behind him are a computer station and bookshelves, notably barren of business books. Yet plaques on the wall attest to his role on the boards of the Wine Institute and the St. Helena hospital, along with dozens of industry kudos and family photos.

RARE BUSINESS SENSE

Roger says that, on occasion, he reads business books. "I get a few ideas, some bits and pieces from them," he casually notes. "I've read Tom Peters and a few inspirational and motivational types. Ken Blanchard, a few others. They've got some neat things to say. I can't say any one has been a guiding light, but they can be interesting."

To suggest that the Trincheros are not wise in the ways of business is foolish. They epitomize an important breed of corporate myth breakers. Their management style reflects a growing trend in business models, one that rewards the kinder, gentler, principled executive over the unscrupulous, self-centered Sun-tzu warrior. *Saving the Corporate Soul,* by David Batstone, addresses this trend. It promotes several key concepts that seem to emanate naturally from within Trinchero Family Estates. Some of the assets Batstone identifies include valuing the worker ("The worker will be treated as a valuable team member, not just a hired hand") and emphasizing community ("A company will think of itself as part of a community as well as a market"), areas in which the Trincheros clearly took the initiative (Batstone 2002).

One of the books Roger mentions that he owns but has yet to read is *Built to Last,* by James C. Collins and Jerry I. Porras (Collins and Porras 1994). Ironically, the Trinchero family business could have been used as a case study in the book. The authors studied visionary companies—3M, Procter & Gamble, Wal-Mart, and others. The result: They identified a dozen myths about successful businesses, and even though TFE was not part of their sample studies, this rags-to-riches company dramatically bursts the same mythology as these other leading giants.

Roger's and Bob's reactions to a few of the myths reveal much about the way they do business.

MYTH: *It takes a great idea to start a business.*

BOB: It was no great idea. Are you kidding? We questioned our business for the first 30 years.

ROGER: Dad wanted to be his own boss. He could have been a grocery store owner. He started the winery because he wanted to get out of New York. The winery itself could have been anything else, any other business. He wanted the opportunity.

MYTH: *Most successful companies exist first and foremost to maximize profit.*

BOB: No. If that were the case, we'd have closed up shop the day after we got here. Lifestyle was much more important. And family.

ROGER: We've always looked at long-term gains versus short-term profits. In fact, that's how we got ourselves into trouble right now. We projected too far out, building more assets than we needed. So we're looking to liquidate some assets now. We got asset-heavy during a downturn in the market. I'm talking about vineyards and at least one production facility. We have three production facilities, but we need only two. We thought we might move our Sutter Home production to the Lodi area, so we began to build a facility over there. But there was a downturn in the market, for various reasons, and our sales didn't hit their projections. So, as any company would do, you take a look and try to liquidate some of it. It's not that our backs are against the wall. It's just something we need to do to move forward. The problem with the wine industry is you've got to think two or three years ahead of time. So you're always guessing where you're going to be, and sometimes you guess wrong. Fortunately, as a privately held company, we answer only to ourselves. We can react to changes in the marketplace fairly quickly.

MYTH: *The most successful companies focus primarily on beating the competition.*

ROGER: No, we're just doing our own thing. We want to beat ourselves, to outdo ourselves from the previous year.

BOB: We do track our competitors; we want to know what they're up to. But we don't really go after them.

ROGER: We're not concerned about what they're doing. But we are interested in knowing what they're doing, because a lot of times we have to react in order to move our business ahead. But it's not a matter of wanting to sell more than Mondavi or Beringer; we just want to sell more than we did last year. Improve our profitability. We just want to better ourselves. We focus on beating ourselves.

Another myth concerns the idea that a company becomes visionary through vision statements. But, say the myth busters, vision is the way you do business every day, at all times. In the case of TFE, the Trincheros have a vision statement, a mission statement, and a list of core values, but these were drafted long after the company became successful—in 1993.

Under the guidance of IBM, the Trincheros hammered out their personal business credo. "They acted as facilitators. We had the family and a few key players, like the vice presidents there, at the Victorian," says Roger. "Together we worked out a vision statement, a mission statement, and the corporate values. We sat down, started talking, and they just developed."

TRINCHERO FAMILY ESTATES
VISION STATEMENT

To be a leader in the wine industry by providing our customers with products of high value while maintaining integrity and family traditions.

MISSION STATEMENT

To attain long-term growth and profitability through the production and sale of high-quality wine and food products for the consumer, guided by our commitment to company values.

VALUES

Integrity: Maintenance of high moral standards, including honesty, trust, and courage of conviction.

Respect for the Individual: To recognize commitment and achievement of each individual, and to consider their ideas, rights, and contributions as vital to the success of the company.

Quality: To take all steps necessary to ensure that Trinchero Family Estates is a benchmark for excellence, consistency, and customer responsiveness in production, sales, and marketing of all Trinchero Family Estates products.

Financial Success: To provide sufficient returns on investments to ensure growth and longevity of the company for the future of the "Trinchero Family Estates Family."

Family: To perpetuate the family atmosphere throughout the entire Trinchero Family Estates organization.

Commitment: To inspire the day-to-day contribution of personal and company goals.

RETROSPECT AND HINDSIGHT

Every business, even the most successful, has failures, and the savviest executives are the ones that turn a failed venture into a positive learning event. When the question of corporate failures comes up, Bob and Roger laugh. "We've had a few of them," they say.

"One of those, I think, was Portico," says Roger. "This was around 1998. When the marketing people at the time came to us and said we need to have flavored White Zinfandel, my heart of hearts said don't do this. But they were very convincing. And it was something we were going to sell at a higher price than our regular White Zinfandel, because it was an added value. . . ."

"That's the thing that got me," Bob interjects.

"Once we got into the market," Roger continues, "all of a sudden we got caught up in an unpredictable controversy about naturally flavored wines and varietals. A segment of the industry felt that no wines with any amount of flavoring added, no matter how small, should be entitled to a varietal designation or vintage date. Portico was 99.8 percent wine, with a little bit of natural fruit flavoring, but several other companies introduced products that were diluted with a lot of water. They were less than 7 percent alcohol, and so did not need to conform to BATF labeling regulations. [FDA, not BATF, regulates alcoholic products with less than 7 percent alcohol and imposes less stringent rules regarding using grape names on the label.] What happened was, we were either going to have to pull Portico off the market or reduce it to under 7 percent alcohol, so the BATF no longer had jurisdiction. We said, we're not going to go to under 7 percent, that's just not our game. We could have been like a Wild Vines or an Arbor Mist, but look what happened to their businesses: They skyrocketed for two years and now they're declining. It's like the wine coolers, it's the same thing."

Bob adds, "We could have done it We certainly have the technology to do it. But we decided, enough's enough."

The line of fruit-flavored wine was discontinued in 1999.

Pasta? Basta!

The Trincheros pulled out of another product line: Sutter Home pasta sauces and vinegars. But in this case, they didn't consider the products a failure. The specialty food business itself, as they were involved in it, simply no longer made sense.

"If we would have gone and built our own food processing plant, I think we could have made it. But since everything had to be farmed out, and all we did was sell it, we didn't know how to do that," explains Bob.

"And not only that," Roger adds, "because we didn't produce it, and we relied on somebody else, we had this cloud of product liability hanging over our head. Every now and then we'd get a letter saying we found this in the pasta sauce, we found that in the pasta sauce. We looked deeper and discovered the margins on food products are very minimal. You've got to sell a lot of volume to make any money. We were one of the highest-priced pasta sauces out there, and we still only made cents on a case. When we looked at the amount of money we made and the potential liabilities and damage it could have done to our core brand name, Sutter Home, we said, it's not worth it. That's why we got out. It put our wine business in jeopardy."

Soléo Revisited

"One new thing we didn't quite hit on was a chillable red wine called Soléo," Roger admits, as if perplexed. "It was a great idea when we first came out with it. But we didn't package it properly; then, when we did get the packaging right, the whole market had changed. And that's something we've struggled with. We even got into flavors with Soléo. We quickly got out of that though. We still sell Soléo, but now only the red and the white. We continue to sell it in pockets around the country, but it just never took off like I thought a chillable red wine could take off. It just never did. What's come on the scene in a big way is white Merlot, which is really a rosé. That's your chillable red wine, and it's selling very well."

Upbeats

"On the other side of the coin, we've got some tremendous successes," Roger notes. "Like the single-service 187s. We continue to grow that business. With our alcohol-free wines under the Fre label, we dominate that market with 70 percent of the sales. That's 250,000 cases." And, as always, White Zinfandel continues to sell. Roger and Bob admit it's hard to anticipate the market, and surprises don't always mean failures. "But then you get something that you think, well, okay, we'll try it—and it becomes a big success, like our Sycamore Lane. Sycamore Lane is a brand we sell strictly on-premise, as in restaurants. We don't sell it off-premise, in retail stores, like we do Sutter Home. And many restaurants and caterers are looking for wines that you can't find in the store, that don't have a retail price visible to the consumer. Sycamore Lane wines are high-quality wines at good prices that they can turn around and sell at even better prices. So they make good profit on their money, and they sell good wine. That's what happened with Sycamore Lane, and it came out of nowhere. We sell 300,000 cases of that a year."

15

The Big Squeeze and the Corporate Crush

Making a buck in the wine industry, including in Napa Valley, has become less about gentlemen farmers and boutique wineries and more about the big corporate squeeze—on both domestic and global levels.

Part of what the industry experiences now is backlash from the boom days of the 1990s, when sales and profits were flush. But that era, following on the heels of the 1980s, when sales declined, was more of an irregularity than the norm. Until 1998, most of that decade's California vintages were exceptional. Later years were not as good, but in Australia, Italy, and other parts of the world, the harvests produced some very fine wines at extremely affordable prices. The dot-com phenomenon also boosted wine sales in the 1990s. A lot of young zillionaires in major metropolitan areas spent hundreds of dollars on bottles of wine at trendy restaurants.

Given today's influences of consolidation and globalization, will the pendulum swing back in California's, and Napa Valley's, favor?

FROM GLOOM TO BOOM?

On the domestic front, wineries faced a particularly sour environment since the start of the millennium. A grape glut choked small and large companies, leading to price wars. A weak economy resulted in decreased restaurant and tourism revenues. Other challenges included globalization, a rise in imports, and consolidation among wineries, retailers, and distributors.

Despite the doom-and-gloom headlines of 2002, which forecast rough times ahead, the actual figures are much more optimistic. California wineries may not have made as much profit, because of discounting, but they shipped a record 463 million gallons, up 3 percent in 2002 from the previous year, worth an estimated $14 billion at retail. In addition, U.S. wine exports (of which California supplies 95 percent) were up by 2 percent. On the downside, imports into the United States climbed to 25 percent of the total market, from about 17 percent the year before.

These numbers reflect industrywide trends, but actual results vary from winery to winery. Even among similar products, some wineries experienced robust sales while others declared bankruptcy, suggesting that the intangibles of strong branding, marketing, and good distribution may be the edge in an otherwise level playing field.

Much of California winery gains were made precisely because of the grape glut, which sparked a run on low-priced blends for the consumer, as in the "Two Buck Chuck" phenomenon of Charles Shaw wines. An explosion of brands, domestic and imported, also increased competition and contributed to pricing discounts. Finally, with a weak economy and rising costs everywhere else, consumers delighted in finding good wines at reasonable prices. As a result of these factors, the largest wine segment, that of wines $7 and under, grew 1.5 percent in 2002—a significant amount, given that these wines account for 70 percent of all California table wines.

The unusual confluence of these factors may not repeat itself in the coming years, at least not to the same degree. Growers pulled out vines and reduced planting, but some industry soothsayers predict harvests in the next few years will be back to normal, and in some cases even below normal, causing increased demand for grapes. Other analysts call this wishful thinking, predicting that supply and demand will remain imbalanced, because tens of thousands of acres are still coming on line, and a huge amount of acreage began to bear fruit just in the past few years. Whichever directions the harvests go, the economies of scale are mushrooming to the point where every winery, no matter what its size, must alter the ways it does business.

The Mondavi Barometer

In 2002 and early 2003, some major players in the wine industry made dramatic and occasionally questionable moves: Gallo bought two wineries to gain a presence in Napa Valley, but the following year dropped from largest to second winery in the world after Constellation's purchase of Australia's BRL Hardy. Fred Franzia gained notoriety for retailing $1.99 "Charles Shaw" wines that received decent reviews and flew off the shelves, sparking a trend for cheap blends from coast to coast. Francis Ford Coppola paid a record price for vineyard land, while his Napa Valley neighbor, Robert Mondavi, saw earnings peak and then plummet.

Robert Mondavi Corporation—arguably the most iconic Napa Valley winery—is publicly traded, though the family still controls 92 percent of the voting shares. The company's shift from record profits in 2001 to a steep decline in 2003, which led to laying off workers and streamlining operations, stunned the industry, the valley, and no doubt its stockholders. As the media reported:

"October 19, 2001—Mondavi uncorks record earnings: Oakville vintners The Robert Mondavi Corp. posted record 2001 first fiscal quarter shipments and earnings for the period ended Sept. 30. Net income grew 22 percent to $11.3 million, compared to $9.3 million for 1999's corresponding period (*San Francisco Business Times*).

"March, 28, 2003—Changes at Robert Mondavi: Citing a weak economy, an oversupply of grapes, intense price competition, as well as increased buyer power at the trade level, Robert Mondavi says this week it expects to report a loss for the current third quarter and said it will cut ten percent of its workforce—roughly 90 employees [including several senior executives]" (*Wine Business Insider*).

The same factors affecting the Robert Mondavi winery are pervasive throughout the Napa Valley and influence the entire California wine industry. According to a corporate press release, the company identified three major factors that negatively affect its business: (1) a weak U.S. economy, which has depressed the travel and entertainment sector and dampened demand, especially for high-end wines; (2) an oversupply of grapes, which leads to intense price competition and a proliferation of new brands; and (3) increased buying power at the trade level. According to R. Michael Mondavi, chairman of the board, "We believe these three factors will be present for a while and we will not see relief from the intense competition until there is a material change in at least one of them."

The Trincheros face these same factors, and they also realize that successful businesses must occasionally redefine what they do and evolve with the currents of change. Many analysts believe that Robert Mondavi Corp. is doing precisely the right thing by restructuring. Essentially, it's a strong company, and by adapting to the newly evolving marketplace, it will probably become even stronger. Whether TFE can follow suit is more difficult to predict, because, unlike the publicly traded Robert Mondavi Corp., its books and its profits are private.

All Gluts, No Glory

The glut of California grapes that hit the market in 2002 stems from overplanting in the 1990s, when Napa Valley and other grape-growing counties were heady with demand. One result of a grape glut is that better quality grapes become available at a lower cost, which means better bargains for consumers, but fewer profits for wineries.

"What we had to do this past year was unbelievable," says Bob in early 2003. "Too much wine, too many grapes. We took 2000 tons of Cabernet and put it into White Zinfandel. That would only extend my White Zinfandel two or three weeks of sales, but it would extend my Cabernet three months. So you start doing stuff like that to shorten the release date. We started the year with 7 million gallons too much of wine. But we'll be in a deficit by next September. We paid some of our growers a year and half's production just to graft over to another variety, Pinot Grigio, in the central coast—about 500 acres.

Overplanting is not uncommon, and as an agricultural business, the wine industry absorbs the fluctuations cyclically, balancing out every few years. But the recent glut came at a particularly bad time. "The oversupply hit right at the moment of an economic downturn, on the heels of 9/11, when people stopped going out to restaurants for a long period," explains Rob Celsi, vice-president of strategic brand development. "It's like the movie *The Perfect Storm:* All of these things lined up at the right point, and a catalyst, an unknown like 9/11, hits right in the middle of an oversupply in our industry."

Despite the industry's 2002 glut of wines on the shelf and an oversupply of grapes, Celsi says he doesn't have to worry too much about competition at the distributor level. "We are blessed with great distribution," he says of Trinchero Family Estates, "because of Sutter Home and the length of time we've been around. It's a known brand name. We are well prepared to ride out any oversupply." Unfortunately, the smaller Napa Valley wineries can't make the same claim, and they're the ones getting knocked out at the distributor level.

Restaurants, particularly upscale venues, suffered hugely from the fallout of 9/11. This in turn hurt winery sales, but TFE was only minimally affected by the downturn in restaurants. "Most of our sales are done in grocery stores and independent retailers," says Celsi. "The impact came when brands that relied solely on white-tablecloth restaurant sales all of a sudden had their revenue restricted severely. Now they need an outlet for their products, so they drop their prices and sell to supermarkets or larger chains where they didn't sell before. Once these wines become cheaper, the customer says, why would I buy my old brand at $16 if that other higher-aspirational brand is now $16? I'll buy it instead. So the guy who sells his wines at $16 says, maybe I got to be at $12, the guy at $12 goes to $7. The guy at $7 says, 'Hellooooo, Sutter Home.' And of course Sutter Home can't turn around and say, I'm going to be a jug wine. So it impacts our business in that sense. It's just the juice rollin' downhill."

Bob notes that, in general, California wines are too expensive. "You sell a wine for $50 a bottle, then the grower wants $5,000 a ton, which then makes his vineyard worth $100,000 an acre. If you could only sell that bottle for $2, then his grapes are worth $200 a ton, and the acres are worth $2,000 an acre. Where's it all end? When wines reach $200 to $250 a bottle, then that just goes through the whole system. When one sector goes up, everybody wants their piece."

Indeed, the Napa Valley Grape Growers Association conducts an annual bottle survey and, with that information, sets recommended prices for local growers. Recommendations are based on the average retail cost of wines, market trends, overall sales, farming costs, and the number of acres planted per varietal. For instance, the average retail price for a Napa Valley Cabernet Sauvignon in 2002 was $51.17 per bottle, up over 23 percent from the previous year. But sales overall were down. So, for 2003, the association recommended Napa Valley growers charge between $3,700 and $4,500 per ton of Cabernet Sauvignon grapes, a range similar to that of the previous year. The group says it intentionally did not raise the price in an effort to "make sure our recommendations are kept in check with the current economic climate and wine sales." Thus, as Bob explained, the prices the wineries pay for grapes, especially in Napa Valley, are tied to retail pricing. As wine prices rise, so, too, do grape prices. And, as grape prices rise, so, too, do wine prices.

Celsi looks at the grape glut from another perspective. "This boom-to-bust agrarian concern is something that I don't see changing that much, because the other problem is the production cycle. If I'm making midlevel vodka, my production cycle is 36 hours, and if potatoes are too expensive overseas, I buy rice from South Carolina. I can make alcohol from anything. Grapes, however, hah! I've got a seven-year production cycle. First, I have to plant, then it's three years before I start picking, then five years until I'm on line. I've got to let it age in expensive French oak for another two years, and then bottle it—and then maybe I get a chance to market it. Seven-year turnaround. You know banks *love* those types of production cycles," he says sarcastically, shaking his head. "So all of these things make our industry very unique compared to any other industry in the country—and prone to its own set of problems.

"Now that will all change," Celsi says, referring to the current glut. "In three or four years, I'll tell you a completely different story. There's a fruit shortage, we can't find fruit everywhere, margins are pressured because I've got to pay more for grapes. Jeez, if I only had another hundred thousand cases we'd be on top of the world. I've been in this business and at this company long enough to see that happen a couple of times. Like clockwork," Celsi says with confidence, "it will happen again."

Consumer Profile

Bob outlines the crux of the problem. "The percentage of wine-drinking adults is not going up. A look at wine-drinking and production statistics underscores the peculiarities of the U.S. wine industry and its consumers:

- Barely 10 percent of adults in the United States consume 86 percent of all the wine according to a 2002 report by *Adams Wine Handbook*. Other reports estimate 16 percent drink 88 percent of the wine.
- The United States ranks third in total wine consumption, after France and Italy. But the United States is thirty-fourth in per capita consumption, with two gallons of wine per person, according to the Wine

Institute's figures for 1999. (Americans drink 22 gallons of beer per person.)

- Rankings of other countries' per capita consumption include Latvia, in thirty-fifth place, Germany, in seventeenth place, while the European nations of Luxembourg, France, Italy, and Portugal hold the top four positions, at between 13 and 16 gallons per person.
- In 2001, California wines accounted for 70 percent of the United States market, or 387 million gallons. In the United States, table wines from all sources totaled 504 million gallons in 2001, dessert wine was 34 million gallons, and sparkling wines were 25 million gallons, according to the Wine Institute. The 2002 retail value of all wine sold in the United States is estimated at $19.8 billion, an increase of more than 4 percent from 2000. The United States ranks fourth in wine production, lagging behind Italy, France, and Spain.

Defining the Market

While wine companies consolidate, Americans, especially baby boomers, are trading up in terms of wine quality as the prices for good wines go down. In the superpremium segment, no single firm dominates the market. Yet, as buyers undergo maturation, the market faces saturation. It seems everyone wants to corner the superpremium market. Meanwhile, a more diverse drinking audience waits to be reached.

"The biggest challenge the industry faces now," observes Roger Trinchero, "is that we have a consumer base that's getting both older and more ethnically diverse. Not to be crass about it, but pretty soon the baby boomers will start disappearing. We have to find ways to popularize wine to a new generation of consumers who are spending money on craft beers and tequila."

It's not simple a matter of redirecting consumers from one form of alcohol to another. Bob outlines the wine industry's hurdle. "Nearly half of Americans don't drink at all. Of those who do drink, a preponderance doesn't drink wine, or are just occasional consumers. Just 20 to 25 percent of Americans drink wine, and only a small number of them drink wine more than once a week."

"Wine has low category penetration," says Rob Celsi. "How to get more people to drink wine—that's always been the holy grail for this industry."

According to Bob, every winery has a goal to increase the overall market of wine drinkers. "That's why we have the Wine Institute and Napa Valley Vintners Association," he says, "to help promote wine. Gallo has promoted wine for years. They've probably created more wine drinkers than any other winery, and they also ship more wine than any other winery."

Cultural groups are new targets. "The two fastest-growing markets, certainly here in California, are the Hispanics and Asians. "If you go back to their countries, they don't have a history of wine consumption. So what you have to do is figure out how you can sell wine to them. But don't forget that half of American adults don't drink any alcohol, which is kind of weird. I mean, why? There are, of course, religious differences and health reasons—but half? And that number hasn't changed much in the past 60 years. So we always have half of this country that doesn't care for beer or anything, no alcohol whatsoever, and the other half that drinks all the alcohol. But the people who move into this country—how do you get them to drink wine? I have no idea. We're so fractionalized that it's very, very difficult. The wine industry never has had, and certainly doesn't have now, a coherent strategy for addressing those groups."

The trick, it seems, is to develop a taste for wine among the non-Caucasian populations, whether they're African American, Asian, or Hispanic. A key point made at the 2002 Wine Industry Financial Symposium was that wineries have been slow to recognize the growth of Hispanic wine drinkers. Yet, according to Univision, the nation's largest Spanish-language television network, more than 25 percent of Hispanics over the age of 21 enjoy drinking wine. Unfortunately, the industry has done little to capitalize on this growth opportunity, even failing to employ Spanish-language advertising campaigns.

Some believe that the real issue centers on wine being class-based. That is, the more affluent people become, the more they gravitate to lifestyles that include and place a positive value on drinking wine. That may change, though, as finer wines become more affordable for mainstream income brackets and as Americans experiment with and discover wines that suit their palates. During Prohibition, wine consumption increased because alcohol was restricted. If the forces of globalization and consolidation make good wines available at costs comparable to, or lower than, beer and other popular alcoholic drinks, the wine industry could experience a boom. But not without reinforcing what many feel is an unfortunate by-product: homogenization.

GLOBALIZATION: NOT IN MY BACKYARD

I am not sure that I like the globalization that is going on in the wine industry. The end result of the huge acquisitions may be driven, heaven forbid, to producing huge quantities of wines that will have the broadest market (profit) appeal, while neglecting the fascinating uniqueness of wines that only smaller producers can craft.—George

Starke, "Up and Down the Wine Roads," *St. Helena Star,* November 15, 2001.

The overriding factors pressuring the wine industry as a whole are globalization and consolidation. Combine these with foreign competition, the idiosyncrasies of wine industry regulations, fluctuating domestic and foreign economies, and unforeseeable agricultural events, and the $50 billion U.S. wine industry starts seeming increasingly fragile, especially for the wineries that have remained independent.

"With all the consolidation, TFE is really one of the last few large winery families still running their own business independently," says Celsi. "There aren't many of us left. I'm very happy that we're not some international conglomerate whose only concern is quarterly returns. Consolidation has a tendency to do that. Consolidation is usually the inevitable conclusion of any type of segment where margins initially are rich and barriers to entry are usually pretty low."

Unlike other wine-growing areas, Napa Valley is almost too expensive, with too valuable an image, to succumb to external pressures. "Napa Valley is probably the least affected by globalization because it has such a high prestige level," Bob notes. "The business will move with the economy. In other words, if the economy is down, maybe my wine's not selling for $200, it sells for $100 now. The economy gets better, and we're back to $200. The people hurt most by this are the Central Valley growers, wineries, and larger producers. They're the ones that will feel the global impact . . . these little wineries that have only 1,000 or 2,000 cases per year."

Roger picks up the thought ". . . Or even up to 50,000 cases if they have a prestigious name will be fine. The guys that have the biggest problem are the ones with the 100,000 to 500,000 cases per year that are caught in the middle. They're not big enough for the distributors to fall over themselves for, and they may not have the prestige, the cachet card to play, so they're stuck in the middle. And this middle-range category is getting larger," Roger adds. "A year from now, that middle ground may range from 100,000 cases to a million cases. And these wineries will be bought up. Examples of ones that have sold recently include Simi, Franciscan, Ravenswood, Louis Martini, Mirassou. These are all in the 150,000- to 500,000-case range. Franciscan was about 400,000."

Bob agrees. "As Roger said, the middle is getting bigger. So now, a million-case winery is considered a midsize winery. It's not a big winery anymore. But it used to be. I mean, we're almost a ten million case winery, and someday we might be in that middle range, too."

BRAND-BUYING BY THE BULK

"The only way public company wineries can grow," explains Bob, "is to buy other wineries. That's the only way they can increase their market share. Because when they report a 2 percent increase or a 1 percent increase, shareholders don't like that. They like 8 percent, maybe even double-digit growth. But they're not getting it because the market's not expanding that fast, so they have to steal it from somebody—or buy another winery. Those wineries with the 250,000 to a million cases, they're really vulnerable for takeover. When you buy such a winery, you've got an instant million-case increase."

Since the overall consumption of wine is barely increasing, the primary way for wine companies to increase their share of the pie is to gobble up other companies. Not only has this happened, but also the pace of these mergers and acquisitions is quickening as never before. Although the Trincheros maintain a sense of security because they are, in a sense, a big enough ship to ride out the storm, the combination of factors, including economic downturn, consolidation, and aggressive marketing and distribution on a global scale, causes many smaller wineries to say *"basta!"* and throw in the towel.

August 2000 saw a single week of major global-merger mania: Australia's Foster's Brewing Group bought Beringer Wine Estates for $1.5 billion, and Canada's Vincor International bought R.H. Phillips for $92 million. Two days later, The Wine Group attempted to grab half a dozen of Sebastiani's high-volume brands in a deal worth more than $300 million. That deal fell through, but in the end, Canandaigua wound up as the buyer instead. Today, Canandaigua is part of Constellation Wines, whose 2003 purchase of Australia's BRL Hardy Wines makes it the world's largest wine company. Gallo now ranks number two, and no doubt the global winery scorecard will change again. For the big fish, family-run wineries are vulnerable prospects, simply because these smaller wineries lack the ability to compete by themselves in the megamarketplace. In September 2002, Modesto-based E.&J. Gallo Winery departed from its previous pattern of building brands from the vine up: The company bought a direct presence in Napa Valley with its purchase of the Louis M. Martini Winery in St. Helena, a deal that included the Martini brand, the winery, and more than 600 acres of vineyards in Napa and Sonoma counties. Founded in 1933, the Martini family had run the very well respected winery until its sale to Gallo. They cited market downturn and competition from bankrolled consolidated wineries as their reasons for selling out.

Just two weeks after the Martini deal was announced, Gallo (then the world's largest winery) also acquired the Mirassou wine brand in Santa Clara County, hiring three members of the sixth-generation Mirassou family to assist in marketing. But unlike the Martini deal, Gallo bought only the Mirassou brand name, not the winery or vineyard assets. The Mirassous, who have made wine in Santa Clara County since 1854, are America's oldest wine-making family. With Gallo's marketing and distribution resources behind them, the Mirassous can continue to make wines without fear of bankruptcy, a fate suffered recently by several smaller wineries that lack prestigious names. Mirassou may even expand. As Heather Mirassou told the *Modesto Bee* on September 21, 2002, they can now reach the next level with the help of Gallo's added marketing and distribution muscle.

CONSOLIDATION

The Trinchero move from mom-and-pop winery to corporate giant reflects what's happening today on a fast-paced, global scale. As they grew, the Trincheros hired MBAs, financial advisors, marketing professionals, ad execs, and other experts to make decisions for the business rather than rely on gut feelings and their own judgments as they once had. This is normal, but in such highly competitive conditions, even the smaller wineries now make such transitions just to stay in the game, while others have cratered into bankruptcy.

Wine columnist Dan Berger has tracked the Trincheros closely over the years. As he notes, "There have been times when they've made some decisions that were strictly oriented toward the bottom line, but as a wine company you've got to do that if you're going to survive without a public offering. The bottom line for wine companies these days is, can you survive the pressures of corporate America? Diageo, Allied Domecq, Canandaigua, Gallo. These are companies that have vast resources. Every one of them has as a goal—if they'd acknowledge it publicly, but they won't—of putting out of business all their competitors. And since Sutter Home is a competitor, and since Sutter Home lacks the financial resources the other companies have had, then their simple act of staying in business and competing on a level playing field—which is not really level—has been a remarkable story of success.

"If you take the top five to seven companies that are corporately owned, you have to say that their staying power is as strong as they want it to be. Canandaigua, Diageo, Foster's Beringer, probably Kendall-Jackson, after you run through the first six or so you realize that they are so overwhelmingly financed, they represent an enormous pressure point for a company like TFE."

Imports on the Rise

Bob is always ready with statistics, not to impress, but because he reads the numbers and uses them to illustrate his viewpoints and guide his decisions. "In 2001, Australia was up 47 percent in imports into the United States, making it the number two imported wine source, knocking France out of the top. Italy is number one."

Indeed, competition from imported wines is causing major migraines for domestic wineries. According to the *Wine Market Report,* imports now account for 25 percent of total U.S. wine sales. In 2002, "imports and fighting varietals walked away with the gains. Imported wines grew at a considerably faster rate (+9.5 percent) versus domestics (+1.7 percent)," according to the 2003 edition of *Adams Handbook Advance,* published by Adams Beverage Group.

Many now find the quality-to-price ratios to be far superior to those of California wines, and even Californian winemakers and drinkers agree.

"It's a very challenging time for all California wineries, inside and outside of Napa Valley, from small producers to megacorps," says Celsi. While California wines are now considered very good to excellent, wines from around the world are as good, and sometimes better, in quality and in value. Certainly, many wine drinkers feel this way about the wines of Australia, New Zealand, and Chile, as well as the traditional wines of Italy and France. The imports also offer a diversity that contrasts with the trend toward homogenization in California wines.

"The big difference is that, truly, we have become globalized as an industry," Celsi adds. "Australia, California, South Africa, South America, New Zealand, as well as the traditionals like France and Italy. I drink from all of those areas. So it's not even competition from within California.

"And you have global companies coming in saying, okay, we'll be global, so if this year Chardonnay is too expensive in California, I'll buy it in Australia, and if it's too expensive there I'll buy it in South America, because most wine drinkers don't really care about where the grapes come from. That hasn't come to pass completely yet, but if I put my one- or two-year goggles on, I think that's coming. What customer wouldn't like to drink from all those countries? It's like a passport in your bottom cabinet.

"I think people will look at Australia as the model and say that American consumers now want to drink around the world. And once you've explored Australia, let's go explore South Africa, then let's go explore Chile. I could see that coming. Sounds like fun doesn't it?"

Aussie Invasion

Has the rise in wines from other companies affected TFE? "Yeah, says Bob," We're being hurt by the imports, especially Australia. Australia is really on a full charge." In 2002, Australian wine imports into the United States surpassed those of the French, making them second only to Italy. (And this was before Americans began to boycott all things French, in reaction to that country's stance on the war in Iraq.)

The country Down Under is also a bit topsy-turvy in its own consumption. "Australia has 19 million people in it," says Bob. "They don't drink wine. They drink beer. They export 80 percent of their total production. I don't know of any other country that exports 80 percent of its wine. Most of them drink their wine. Like Italy, which is also the largest wine-exporting country. I read that in the next five years, the Australians are going to increase their vineyards by 50 percent production."

In 2001, the Trincheros announced a joint venture with Australia's Cabonne Limited to market and sell wines from Reynolds Vineyards in New South Wales. TFE's entry into Australian wines is a conservative and tame step compared to the global reactions of other companies, which have diversified into South America, New Zealand, South Africa, and Europe. Similarly, Australia suffered a shortage of Chardonnay, so it's buying Chardonnay from, not surprisingly, California, primarily for use in its bag-in-a-box wines.

MARKETING AND DISTRIBUTION

The proliferation of imports crowds an already overpopulated domestic market. "There are so many brands, just to get the attention, you have to market on many levels," explains Karla McKee, TFE's director of marketing information. "Because the distributor is presenting your wines to the retail accounts, you have to market to the distributors, so they know how to present your brands and, hopefully, put more attention on your brands. Then, too, there's the retail trade, meaning both restaurants and supermarkets and other channels, because they have so many brands to put on the shelf, and shelf space is precious. It costs money. It's real estate to them. What brands they do feature and support need to be worth their while. And then, finally, you need to market wine to the consumer, who is actually buying it. We really need to market our wines on all three levels."

As opposed to other supermarket products, wine companies are stringently regulated when it comes to promotional practices involving retailers. "Unlike the nonalcoholic products, we're not allowed to pay slotting fees. That's when a brand pays the store for the space of their product," McKee says. "We're also not allowed to do co-op advertising, as when a retailer and a brand split ad costs. And we're not legally permitted to do incentives for the retail trade. So we try to demonstrate how consumers want the brands, how they will buy the brands, how the distributors and retailers will make money with them, and we use consumer data to illustrate the demographics. 'These people are buying our brands and they are also shopping at your store, and these are the people you want to attract to your store, or your restaurant.' Finally, we use point-of-sale materials, which help the retailers sell to the consumer. With all these holdover restrictions from Prohibition, that's really all we're allowed to use as incentives at that level."

The Money in Marketing

Today, in response to increased competition, the larger winemakers are less likely to change the chemistry of a wine than to change their marketing by conducting surveys and adjusting the wine's image to dovetail with selective consumer preferences. Even small boutique wineries in Napa Valley resort to strategic marketing tactics and hire marketing experts, something unheard of before the crunch.

"The wine industry is now founded on sales and marketing," said Gary Heck of F. Korbel & Bros., known for its sparkling wine, in a wine-industry survey (*Strategy and Leadership in the Northern California Wine Industry,* 1998, conducted by Sonoma State University). "It's a people business. Whether you are the owner, manager, or vice president, you have to go out and see the distributors. Things get done because of your willingness to see the buyers."

You schmooze or you lose, in contemporary jargon. And it's not just behind the scenes with distributors where the big players have an edge. The megacorporations have at their disposal enormous resources: larger sales forces, bigger marketing budgets, and greater distribution clout—all key ingredients for success today. As is true of many other industries, the U.S. wine industry relies on a three-tier system of the producer/supplier (such as the winery or importer), the distributor, and the retailer—but other industries don't face the same stringent regulations imposed on the alcoholic beverage industry. By law, a winery may not own or control a company in the distributor or retailer tiers. As a consequence, it's important that a winery have major clout with distributors and strong relationships with the retailers. Schmooze or lose.

With the downturn of the market, some of the smaller, upper-crust wineries have taken up schmoozing. They have to push their wines hard or go soft on their prices. Faced with dropping her Cabernets to below $90 a bottle, as her distributor suggested, Shari Staglin—who with her Silicon Valley husband, a venture capitalist, launched their Staglin Family Winery in Napa Valley in 1985—hit the road instead. As the *Los Angeles Times* reported on January 5, 2003, "This fall, with her suitcases full of Cabernet, Chardonnay and a little Sangiovese tucked in the side pocket, Shari Staglin went on a door-to-door campaign to sell wines from the Staglin Family Vineyard to restaurants and wine stores, dropping her long-standing wine distributor in favor of the personal approach." Staglin succeeded, selling all 5,000 cases at their full price. Other small but upscale wineries are taking similar measures, bombarding posh restaurant owners and managers with personal phone calls, mailers, and visits—not just from sales reps, but from the winery owners themselves.

Innovative Marketing

Though Bob Trinchero jokes about replacing screw caps with corks to infiltrate the Costco market, wines as affordable beverages are popping up in the most pedestrian of places. That icon of mini-mart chains, 7-Eleven stores, displays special informational wine racks to encourage sales of premium wines in the $5 to $10 range, focusing on Chardonnay, White Zinfandel, Merlot, and Cabernet. According to a company spokesperson, 80 percent of all wine is consumed at home. It's also the fasting-growing category of beverages other than soft drinks, so the world's largest convenience retailer, with more than 23,000 stores, eagerly offers its customers a newfound convenience in wine buying. A bottle of premium Cabernet is just a 7-Eleven away. Furthermore, in 2003, the 7-Eleven company dove headfirst into wine sales, launching its own private-label wines under the brand name Regions, starting with Australian Chardonnay and Italian Pinot Grigio, at $4.99 per 375-milliliter bottle.

Wineries want to ramp up mass-market awareness and demand for higher-quality premium wines in other unique ways. Napa Valley's Clos du Val winery has a product-placement deal to feature its wines on the popular HBO series, *The Sopranos*. Even beer-guzzling sports fans receive wine pointers from the servers at Texas Stadium, which resulted in a 16 percent increase in wine consumption during the 2001 Dallas Cowboys season. Is marketing more important than the taste of the product? "No, not at the end of the day," says Celsi. "Marketing can get someone to try a product once, but if it isn't in the bottle vis-à-vis price value, they won't come back again. A good ad campaign will get people to try something, but it won't get someone to buy their product over time. Of course, we are impacted by the vagaries of an agricultural industry subject to a boom-and-bust cycle—for example, now, with the glut. Your marketing tactics change during those time periods. Oversupply equals pricing pressure. You have a choice. You can maintain your share, which means you fight on price wherever you have to. Or you can take the high road and not reduce your price, and watch your share erode."

Which is exactly what Robert Mondavi Corp. did in 2002. Instead of reducing the prices of its wines in reaction to the competition, Mondavi poured more dollars into advertising. Error. It's now shifting those promotional budgets into discounting and restructuring to meet "today's value-conscious consumer."

Celsi tries to explain the anomaly. "It's a difficult situation because there are few dominant brands in this industry. There are a multitude of brands and labels out on the shelf for a low-penetration category, vis-à-vis the rest of the population. There is limited brand loyalty. This is an industry that rewards consumer promiscuity. I mean, talk to folks and ask them questions. You're a wine drinker, right? And they say, yeah, I love wine. Well, what do you drink? Do they say a brand? Rarely. They say, I'm a Chardonnay drinker. Oh, that's great. So I say, out of Chardonnays, is there one you like most, one that's your favorite? Oh, I like such and such. Is that the only one? Oh no, I also like this and this . . . What happens is that you end up with five or six brands that are in an acceptable repertoire of brands that go on sale, that you see stacked out on the floor in the supermarket, that you say, jeez, $5.49, too. Maybe I'll like this wine. I'll buy it. No one is going to say, jeez, $5.49—no, my brand is X and I'm gonna pay $2 more because I like that brand. Rarely does that happen. There are few brands that have high levels of loyalty. So, no loyalty in the category, fragmented category without category leaders, and an oversupply—that equals pricing pressure. You can choose to keep your share, or you can choose to take the high road, to oblivion, at times." Nothing is set in stone, and Celsi points out that tactics do change. "Obviously, if you have to fight on price, that pinches your margins, and if you pinch your margins, where is that money going to be made up? Well, that's going to be made up on cost containment, which is code for 'we're not going to spend as much on these discretionary activities.' That may be buildings, that may be trucks, that may be tanks, and it may be advertising. Think of the line item in someone's budget that has a big fat number and that is little understood to begin with. You know, John Wanamaker said it: 'Half of my advertising dollars are wasted, I just don't know which half.' Boom! Just when they tell you in classic marketing that in a down market you advertise even more—because you'll have even greater share when you come out of it—the pressure to *not* do that is greatest. And it's widespread through any industry."

Full Steam Ahead

Ultimately, many analysts believe the industry will stratify into two camps: on one level, a large pool of mass-market, affordable wines sold in supermarkets, priced under $12, with the $6-and-under fighting varietals and blends being the biggest volume; on the other, small volumes of ultra-premium, specialty wines from Napa Valley and other elite growing areas, sold on premise, in tasting rooms, through wine clubs, and to connoisseurs, at $30 and above.

The little guys may be the engine that drives Napa Valley, but it's the giants with their vast resources, like Gallo and Constellation, that now fuel the industry. In the end, the Trincheros may survive and even thrive in the middle simply because they're their own bosses and have the flexibility to do things their own way, however unorthodox that may be.

16

Onward

From courtly Shakespearean dramas to Schwarzenegger action flicks, the most compelling stories are the ones whose characters change over time.

Long perceived by themselves and others as outsiders in America's wine paradise, the Trinchero family in recent years has broken bread with Napa Valley's fine-wine community—first through the success of their upscale Trinchero brand and, most recently, by chairing the 2003 Napa Valley Wine Auction, Napa's famed annual wine soiree.

At the same time, their company has evolved from an upstart mom-and-pop operation (one that has improbably managed, over the course of two decades, to regularly kick sand in the faces of the big players) to a thriving business endeavoring to find its place in the new corporate, global wine village. As Bob, Roger, and Vera—the Trinchero generation that made Sutter Home a household name and introduced millions of Americans to premium wine—approach retirement and contemplate what comes next, questions of succession, transition, and even survival of their family winery loom large.

NAPA SOCIETY AND
VALLEY POLITICS

Despite their newfound success in the Napa Valley fine-wine business, Bob and Roger still appear more comfortable with the folks on the bottling line than in high society. "Absolutely right," agrees Roger with emphasis. "Because we were on the bottling line a lot longer than we were behind these desks," adds brother Bob.

To some extent, the Trincheros remain removed from Napa Valley's haute lifestyle and social attitudes. Vera says she doesn't mind her anonymity, despite being a leading philanthropist, in the valley, but it appears to rankle. "Lots of people in this valley don't even know I exist," she remarks. " 'Oh, you're Bob and Roger's *sister?*' Yeah."

While the Trincheros are not excluded from Napa Valley society, they're not exactly the debutantes at the ball. The family may claim to prefer being outside the main social circuit, but their comments reveal an ambivalence.

"The wine community here doesn't exclude us. Well, in some ways they do, but they really can't," Bob says, searching to explain the paradox. "It's like, you've got a room with six elephants, and I'm one of them, and the rest are smaller. I'm the biggest elephant in that room, so you can't ignore me. You may not like the fact that I'm in the room, but you can't ignore me.

"Frankly, I don't think people in Napa Valley know what to do with us. They know we've been here forever, but they wish we weren't so . . . *big.*"

Roger chimes in. "They wish our brand wasn't so . . . *everywhere,* so common!"

"That's it," Bob agrees. "You can buy our wines *anywhere,* so they lack that air of exclusivity that has become very important in Napa Valley."

Observes Roger, "I think a lot of Napa Valley people these days are in the wine business to be in the wine business, as a lifestyle. For us, this is a business. Period. We happen to sell wine as our product. We try to do the best we can and be the best producers and sellers of wine that we can be. We'd be doing the same thing if we made widgets."

The Trincheros are astonished at the astronomical prices—up to $250 per bottle—that are commonplace these days for Napa's most-sought-after wines. (Their ultrapremium Trinchero wines, which regularly earn top scores and awards, sell for about $45.)

Their reaction to the high prices probably reflects their upbringing with Mario and Mary, when there was rarely extra money for indulgences. While the Trincheros do enjoy their success—vacations in Hawaii for Bob and Evalyn, ski trips for Roger and his kids, and jaunts to Tahoe for Vera and her pals—they find philanthropy is the best way to spend the riches most other people would lavish on themselves and their families.

That's why they agreed to chair the 2003 Napa Valley Wine Auction, the world's largest charity auction. Because of the Trincheros' commitment to giving, they were willing to promote outrageous wine prices—for a good cause. At the auction, which changes hosts annually, a $250 bottle of wine is a bargain, and tickets cost $2,500 per couple, just to attend.

The 2002 event raised an impressive $6.12 million. However, in 2003, the Trincheros personally brought the Napa Valley Wine Auction tally to an even higher grand total: $6.57 million. Not only did the Trincheros host the 2003 event, they energetically inspired bidders to reach deep into their pockets by setting a personal example: They raised the stakes of the "Bidder's Brand" lot, in which the winners become instant vintners, procuring everything needed to create 300 cases of fine Napa Valley Cabernet Sauvignon in their own name, including the grapes, wine-maker, French oak barrels, label design, marketing plan, bottling and packing, and membership in the prestigious Napa Valley Vintners Association.

A Texas couple, John and Tamra Gorman, won the Bidder's Brand lot with a bid of $320,000, making them the top bidders of the day—but they weren't the auction's biggest donors. The Trinchero family, just prior to the lot's opening bid, stunned the crowd by offering to match the lot's winning bid up to $1 million, thereby surpassing the previous record of $700,000 set three years prior. Another patron generously donated an additional $25,000 to the Bidder's Brand lot amount, but the Trincheros weren't sat-isfied with just matching the combined bid. With their typical generosity, they chipped in the remaining $655,000 to reach a record-breaking bid of $1 million, making this the largest winning live-auction lot in the history of the Napa Valley Wine Auction.

Even before the 2003 auction, the Trincheros' magna-nimity did not go unnoticed in Napa Valley. In 1996, Bob Trinchero was named St. Helena Citizen of the Year. In 1998, Vera was named by the California state legislature as Woman of the Year for the state senatorial district encom-passing Napa County. And in May 2003, Bob and his wife Evalyn received doctorates in philanthropy from Napa's Pacific Union College in Angwin.

It's important to understand that what the Tricheros did for the auction was an expression of purely philan-thropic instincts and in no way conflicts with their belief that, charitable donations aside, good wine can and should be made and sold at reasonable—and not overinflated—prices.

MENDING FENCES

The Trincheros' distaste for stratospheric wine prices is tempered by their understanding of the romance of wine and the role it plays in preserving the unique character of Napa Valley. "People spending that amount of money for a bottle of wine are really buying a story in that bottle, an ambience, an experience," Bob says. "But you know what? I don't disparage them. And the reason I don't is, what's the alternative?"

Bob explains an economic irony of the Napa Valley. "If land here is worth $100,000 or more per acre for an agricultural product, is this really agriculture? No, because if it's worth that much, this isn't just agriculture. We paid $5,000 a ton for Cabernet grapes from one grower. He has four and a half acres of land, so we paid him $100,000 for 20 tons. Now, if I went to Nebraska and talked to a corn farmer and told him I just paid $100,000 for what came off four and a half acres, he'd think I was crazy—or a wheat farmer in Kansas . . . or an orange grower in Florida.

"This isn't agriculture. What we have here is a treasure. A delicate one, to be sure. And what's the alternative?" Bob asks, pointing out the window. "If that property out there was only $1,000 an acre, or $500, or whatever corn acreage sells for, there'd be houses on it. But as long as it's worth what it's worth and produces this kind of product, it will always stay in grapes.

"Once you lose the grapes, forget it. That four-lane freeway that ends in Yountville will go all the way to Calistoga, you'll have a BART station in Napa, and we'll become a bedroom community for the Bay Area. On the other hand, we have to pay up to $200,000 for an acre of land."

Not all Napa valley land sells for that much—or that little. In 2002, Napa Valley saw the highest price ever paid in
the New World for vineyard acreage. The record sale was
more than $350,000 per acre, paid by Francis Ford Cop-
pola and a partner, for a historic Rutherford estate adjacent
to Coppola's Niebaum-Coppola winery. Altogether, the
deal included 203 acres, with 110 acres on a slope that's
considered watershed and not likely to be planted, for a
total of $31.5 million.

Napa Valley's Unique Profile

On a global scale, internal Napa Valley issues may seem
minor and inconsequential. But like the creaking sounds of
a bridge when stressed, such tensions forebode increasing
pressures in the entire wine industry. In Napa Valley, though,
the dynamics of real estate, image, tourism, and the environment magnify the scale and impact of just about everything.
They become inflated, like balloons in a Macy's Day parade,
casting huge shadows on the entire terrain simply because of
the enormous degree to which money, history, culture,
tourism, and livelihoods are at stake in Napa Valley.

Napa Valley has a fair share of local concerns and regu-
latory quirks. Issues that pit environmentalists against
wineries are just one type of struggle. In a sense, both sides
want the same thing: to preserve the character and unique
treasure that is Napa Valley. But how best to achieve that
goal, and who will have to give up what, has caused the
stir. Plus, there's added pressure coming from Realtors and
housing demands.

Who Controls the Land?

The $350,000 per acre that Coppola paid isn't typical for
the average Napa Valley vineyard, but even so, the value of

Napa Valley acreage is off the charts compared to vineyards anywhere else in California. Indeed, the land itself is at the heart of Napa Valley's most fervent controversies—how much it costs, who it belongs to, and what can be done with it. Complex environmental issues, in particular, cause heated arguments.

Bob becomes extremely passionate about certain topics, and the Watershed Protection Act, a hot issue in Napa in 2003, is high on his list. "The only way we may lose our treasure is from within. Right now, we have some environmentalists trying to impose setbacks. They want to set our vineyards back some 100 feet or more from a stream. Well, that's ridiculous. There's no science there. It's all emotion. If they can pass that, then that's the beginning of slowly ruining this valley."

Roger elaborates, "What's amazing to me is that you can't put a vineyard near a stream, but you can build a house. This is what concerns me," he says about the proposed act.

"They have to allow that. Because all the homeowners came unglued when the environmentalists proposed the setbacks. 'What do you mean my house can't adjoin a stream?' That's it. Better remove that part of the deal."

"We don't want to alienate voters, only grape growers," Bob adds with wry sarcasm.

"Here's the problem," Bob explains. "The supervisors control the unincorporated areas. But vines don't vote; people vote. Napa and American Canyon are where all the voters are. They're the ones who elect the supervisors, with the exception of the one we elect at the north end in District 3. The people live in the city, yet they elect the supervisor, even though the supervisor controls only the unincorporated areas, which I think is kind of stupid. I think the people in the unincorporated areas should elect the supervisors. But that's not the way it works. Vines don't vote. People vote. So there you are.

"And you know what?" Bob asks with intense conviction. "We've been fighting what is probably just a delaying action. I think it's possible that by the end of this century, there will be no Napa Valley wine industry. It will become a bedroom community for the Bay Area—because the pressure is too great. Just look at the other counties. Marin County is half our size, yet it has four times the amount of people. Sonoma County has four or five times that amount. It's really too bad. And it's not coming from the outside. It's from the inside where it will happen." (At the time of this writing, the fate of the Watershed Protection Act remains unresolved.)

Napa "Grandfathers"

Along with environmental issues, another major controversy in Napa Valley is over the use of the Napa name.

Because Napa Valley is California's most prized viticultural area, the Napa name alone may be as valuable as any ton of grapes grown there, as exemplified by controversies over the use of brand names that incorporate the Napa Valley appellation. In 1986, the federal Bureau of Alcohol, Tobacco and Firearms (BATF) adopted a truth-in-advertising regulation hailed by Napa Valley vintners as a means of protecting the value of the Napa name, or appellation. The regulation stipulates that at least 85 percent of the grapes in a wine identified on its label as coming from a specified viticultural area, such as Napa Valley, must come from that region. However, a grandfather clause allows brands established prior to July 7, 1986, to continue using names that originally incorporated appellation names, regardless of whether their wines contain any grapes from those appellations.

While Sutter Home may identify itself in the fine print on its labels as a Napa Valley winery, even though it uses few Napa Valley grapes, a Sutter Home wine cannot bear the Napa Valley appellation unless it contains 85 percent Napa Valley grapes. (The ultrapremium wines of the Trinchero brand carry a Napa Valley appellation because they're made entirely from Napa Valley grapes.)

The grandfather exemption, however, permits companies like Fred Franzia's Bronco Wine Co., makers of Charles Shaw, to bottle and market non-Napa wines using purchased, grandfathered brands that incorporate Napa appellations, such as Napa Ridge and Rutherford Vintners. (Rutherford is a recognized subappellation within Napa Valley.) While Franzia can do this legally, it's a festering wound among Napa vintners who don't want the value of the Napa name diluted. Some especially militant Napa vintners would like to see the valley's wineries restricted to using only Napa grapes.

Roger speaks earnestly: "Wineries like ours, which have longtime roots in Napa Valley—going back to the days when it didn't mean much to be here in terms of consumer perception—are now looked at differently. People say, hey, wait a minute, you shouldn't bring wine in here to bottle if it's not from Napa Valley grapes. That sort of thinking is generated to a great extent by Johnny-come-latelies, new winery owners who came here and started to dictate how this valley should be run.

"But this is our *home*. We've been here since 1948. We are able to produce not only Napa Valley wines, we produce wines from other areas. We have vineyards all over California, we contract grapes from all over California, we bring them in here, we crush them, we produce the wines, we bottle them down in Napa at Green Island Road, and we ship them out. And it's entirely legal."

THE TARNISH OF WHITE ZINFANDEL

Sutter Home may have a long history in Napa Valley, as do Beringer and Mondavi, but unlike those prestige wineries, which also market inexpensive brands, its success with bargain-priced wines, especially White Zinfandel, has been a double-edged sword.

"Our success has also been a curse in some respects," Roger confirms. "Because we sell wines of great value, people think they can't be that good. Some people don't want to buy a wine and bring it over to someone's home if doesn't seem expensive. So they think, I'm not going to bring Sutter Home Gewürztraminer to my friend's house. It's only $4.99. Even though it's the best Gewürztraminer value in the state, it doesn't have the image.

"And therein lie a lot of the problems we face as a family business: We have built our business on a quality-versus-price relationship, providing value to the consumer. It's difficult to compete today with the multinationals, companies that have a lot more money to work with at those price points. And we don't have the right image to compete on the higher end, because people have this perception of Sutter Home as a value-priced wine and that's it. It's difficult, even with our other wines, to step into the next price category. We did it with Trinchero, we did it with Montevina, we're doing it with Trinity Oaks, but it's difficult. And even with Trinchero, although our wines are as good as many of the so-called cult wines here in the valley, we don't get the same respect they do, simply because we're Sutter Home.

"In some respects," Roger concludes, "we're the victim of our own success."

GAME PLANS

"We've done a couple of things that have positioned us well for growth over the next few years," Roger says. "Number one is to shore up the Sutter Home business and make sure we pay attention to it and increase it. Even if it's only a 1 or 2 percent growth each year, with such a large base, that's significant.

"Number two is Trinity Oaks, a higher-priced brand that's moving into a lot of markets as a domestic alternative to midpriced imported brands. We're increasing the impact of both our Trinity Oaks and Sutter Home brands by adding Pinot Grigio to the mix, which will boost our sales." Roger's faith in Pinot Grigio is well founded. An analysis of 2001 wine sales reveals that Italian Pinot Grigio is now the top-selling imported table wine in the United States, exceeding imported Merlot and Chardonnay, with growth expected to exceed 6 million cases in 2003.

"Our Montevina brand continues to grow in its price category, as does our Trinchero brand. And we have an Australian brand, Reynolds Vineyards, which is a joint venture with an Australian company. Those wines are doing very well, because they're top quality and they exploit the tremendous interest American consumers have in Australian wines. We're also looking at another joint venture involving Italian wine.

"We're positioned at just about every price level and with all the major wine types. By doing that, we're ready for any growth spurts that may occur in any of those categories."

Planned Growth

Is there a risk of diversifying too much? "Yes, absolutely," Roger says. "You end up overloading your sales force and losing focus on priorities. We're careful about that, and we've actually turned down a couple of opportunities that we felt were too much. We recently had discussions with an Argentine company that wanted to spend significant dollars to have us sell their wines in the United States, but we didn't want to take that on, simply because there are already too many irons in the fire. Right now, we've got what we want in terms of our brand lineup, and we think that's enough for our sales force. You get too diversified and you lose your focus. Then all the brands suffer."

Some companies spew out new wines like bullet shells from a Gatling gun, particularly the megacorporations with seemingly unlimited funds. The Trincheros take a more conservative approach, as Roger explains: "We don't come out with a new wine unless we're sure it's going to sell. Pinot Grigio is one example.

"We had Pinot Grigio out for more than two years with the Montevina brand, but we just couldn't access enough grapes to expand. Now we have some contracts in place with growers, and we've planted our own Pinot Grigio vines. That's all coming into production, so we're able to produce Pinot Grigio for the Trinity Oaks and Sutter Home brands."

Have the Trinchero fine-wine brands overcome the stigma of White Zinfandel? "Well, we're getting much better scores in *Wine Spectator* and other wine magazines because of Trinchero, Montevina, and Reynolds. Our wines are getting scores in the 90s now, so maybe perceptions are starting to change."

Expansion and diversification aside, every smart businessperson understands that there are some things in a business you should not change. What should not change at TFE? Without blinking, thinking, or even breathing, Bob answers, "Our focus on Sutter Home. It's 95 percent of our sales. It's our core brand."

In Conclusion

Most privately held wineries have traditionally been small entrepreneurial businesses that are distinctly different from their publicly traded counterparts, both structurally and in scope. The Trincheros' company is privately held, but doesn't operate like a small business. For their first 35 years, the Trincheros bought all of their grapes from suppliers, never owning a single acre of land themselves. Since then, they've aggressively purchased large tracts of land, converted them to vineyards, and are cultivating their way to self-sufficiency. They've also invested heavily in improved facilities, state-of-the-art processing equipment, laboratory technology, and enhanced bottling efficiency. But knowing when to reverse course is as important as knowing when to expand. When times got tough, they prudently pulled back, refocusing on their strengths and discontinuing projects as needed to ensure the prosperity of the company. Yet, unlike so many large corporations, they have not compromised their ethics. They place tremendous value on their employees, their community, and their family ties.

In retrospect, the Trincheros enjoy a flexibility that most publicly held corporations lack. Time after time, their actions, though they have run contrary to conventional wisdom, have been catalysts in creating their success, particularly their invention and promotion of Sutter Home White Zinfandel. "Our willingness to take risks has its basis in the fact that we're family owned," explains Roger Trinchero. "We don't have to answer to corporate shareholders. We look at everything in terms of where we want to be down the road, not what we want to accomplish by the end of the year."

The Trincheros entertained the possibility of selling out to a global corporation, suggesting that if the right offer comes along in the future, the family might consider it. Vera works at the winery part-time, Roger would like to spend more time with his kids, and Bob, though he says he's not going anywhere, is at the age where his cadre of vintner buddies is diminishing; they're either selling their wineries, retiring, or passing away. As successors to the throne, nephews Tony and Bobby Torres have many assets, but question whether they're prepared to lead the winery.

Bob speaks matter-of-factly about the future. "First of all, we're in the wine business, and it's a business. So we will look at any proposition, and if it's good for the family, which is what we always look at, we'll consider it. But we're not looking to sell. There are very few potential buyers for Sutter Home. I mean, we're that big, and we're really not that interested in buying other wineries. I think we'll just continue to do what we've been doing."

Whatever happens to Trinchero Family Estates concerns more than just the money involved. Bob, Roger and Vera care about their business and their workers, just as their father Mario did years ago. "He had a passion for the wine business," muses Roger. "He enjoyed working those long hours because it was something he really wanted to do, and he felt he was doing it for himself and his family, not for somebody else. That's instilled in us, too—we like doing it for ourselves, our family, and the people who work for us."

In a world of corporate consolidations, downsizing, and financial scandals, genuine integrity appears to be a rare asset. Mario's sense of values and his hands-on devotion to the company contributed to the Trincheros' success, as did the Trincheros' knack for creating products in sync with consumer tastes and their willingness to take risks and invest in their own intuition and insights, however unorthodox. The megacorps may have vast resources, but they also have more limitations and a nervous reticence about embracing unproven products.

Ask Roger, Bob, and Vera what they think, and they'll calmly tell you, in their typical self-assured yet humble way, that despite the stresses of globalization and consolidation, they haven't changed, and their business is right on track. Their long-standing values and intuition will continue to bring them success for as long as they control the family business. In what direction they'll go remains to be seen. However, given its history, Trinchero Family Estates will no doubt be a challenging force and a winery to watch in the continuing evolution of the global wine world and the future of Napa Valley.

References

Batstone, David, *Saving the Corporate Soul* (New York: John Wiley & Sons, 2002), table of contents.

Bullard, Robyn, "The House That White Zinfandel Built." *Wine Spectator*, vol. 19, no. 3, May 15, 1994, pp. 54, 55.

Cakebread, Sarah, "Our Side of Eden." *Napa Valley News* (www.napanews.com), November 2, 2002.

Caplow, Theodore, Louis Hicks, and Ben J. Wattenberg, "The First Measured Century: An Illustrated Guide to Trends in America, 1900–2000." 2000, PDF file at www.pbs.org/fmc/downloadbook.htm.

Collins, James C., and Jerry I. Porras, *Built to Last* (New York: HarperCollins, 1994), pp. 1, 7, 8, 9, 10.

Conaway, James, *The Far Side of Eden* (Boston: Houghton Mifflin, 2002), p. 194.

Ferguson, Scott, "Trincheros Dismiss Reports of a Deal with Constellation Brands as Rumor," *St. Helena Star* (www.sthelenastar.com), November 15, 2001.

Flamm, Jerry, *Good Life in Hard Times* (San Francisco: Chronicle Books, 1999), p. 21.

Lechmere, Adam, and agencies, "Hardy Shareholders Approve Constellation Merge," *Decanter* (www.decanter.com), March 21, 2003.

Lewis, Oscar, *Sutter's Fort: Gateway to the Gold Fields* (New York: Prentice-Hall, 1966).

Index

About the Authors

KATE HEYHOE is an award-winning online editor, author, magazine writer, and entrepreneur. She and her husband Thomas Way created the Web's first food and wine e-zine in 1994, Global Gourmet (global-gourmet.com). The following year they became partners with America Online, where she featured Julia Child and Jacques Pépin in their online debuts. Her books include *Macho Nachos* (2003), *A Chicken in Every Pot: Global Recipes for the World's Most Popular Bird* (2004), and *Cooking with Kids For Dummies* (1999, foreword by best-selling author Mollie Katzen).

Early on, Heyhoe worked as a food columnist in Texas, where she received a Bachelor in Journalism degree, followed by postgraduate studies in Radio-TV-Film at the University of Texas at Austin. She later became chef-owner of her own restaurant in Italy. She writes for national magazines and speaks frequently at industry conferences, including those of the International Association of Culinary Professionals (IACP), Women Chefs & Restaurateurs (WCR), and the National Association for the Specialty Food Trade (NASFT).

Prior to her publishing activities, Heyhoe worked as a film and TV production manager in Hollywood, where she balanced the creative, financial, and administrative demands of entertainment media. Today, she wines and dines in bucolic Cherry Valley, California, with her husband, six cats and dogs, and intermittent visits by bears, owls, and coyotes.

STANLEY HOCK is a public relations and marketing consultant to some of California's best-known wineries. Before establishing his own business, he served for 13 years as director of communications at Sutter Home Winery in Napa Valley.

During his 25-year career in the California wine industry, Hock has also been a fine-wine retailer and a widely published wine writer. He is the author of *Harvesting the Dream,* a commemorative book chronicling the Trinchero family's 50-plus years in the Napa Valley wine business, and collaborated with renowned cookbook author James McNair on the *Sutter Home Napa Valley Cookbook,* published by Chronicle Books.

A political science major at the University of California at Berkeley during the late 1960s, Hock has an interest in politics, international affairs, and modern literature. He maintains a modest wine cellar in the garage of his home in Kensington, California.